The BUSINESS WRITING WORKBOOK

The BUSINESS WRITING WORKBOOK

A Guide to Defensive Writing Skills

Ian Stewart

Kogan Page

First published in Canada in 1985 by
International Self-Counsel Press Ltd,
North Vancouver, British Columbia

Copyright © International Self-Counsel Press Ltd 1985

This edition first published in
Great Britain in 1987 by Kogan Page Ltd,
120 Pentonville Road, London N1 9JN

New material copyright © Kogan Page Ltd 1987

All rights reserved

British Library Cataloguing in Publication Data

Stewart, Ian
   The business writing workbook: a guide to
   defensive writing skills.
   1. English language — Business English
   2. English language — Writing
   I. Title
   808'.066651021   PE1115
   ISBN 1-85091-309-9

Printed and bound in Great Britain by
Biddles Ltd, Guildford

Contents

1. Introduction — 7
What is defensive writing? 7; Who is this workbook for? 8; How to use this workbook 8; Exercise 1.1 The defensive writing test 9

2. Words — 11
Vocabulary reduction 11; Exercise 2.1 Vocabulary reduction 13; Conciseness 14; Say it more simply 14; Exercise 2.2 Shortening sentences (1) 15; Exercise 2.3 Shortening sentences (2) 17; Exercise 2.4 Reducing standard phrases 18

3. Phrases and Punctuation — 19
Dangling phrases 19; Exercise 3.1 Dangling phrases 20; Punctuation guide 21; Exercise 3.2 Punctuation 24

4. Sentences and Paragraphs — 25
Sentences 25; Exercise 4.1 Eliminating the passive voice 28; Exercise 4.2 Parallel structure 30; Exercise 4.3 Subject and verb agreement 32; Exercise 4.4 The time line (1) 33; Exercise 4.5 The time line (2) 34; Paragraphs 34

5. Memos — 36
Memo checklist 36; The standard memo format 37; Exercise 5.1 Short memo 38; Exercise 5.2 Memo report 39; Steps in memo writing 39

6. Letters — 41
The zero reply principle 41; Exercise 6.1 Letter 42; We and I 42; Exercise 6.2 Rejection letter 44; Rejection letters 44

7. Reports — 46
Parts of a formal report 46; Presentation 50; Exercise 7.1 Report 51

8. General Tips on Writing Office Documents   53
The four steps to good writing 53; Starting sentences for memos and letters 55; Final sentences in memos and letters 56; Tone and effect 58; Poison words 59; Exercise 8.1 Tone and effect 60; The master document 61

9. Forms and Manuals   63
Forms 63; Exercise 9.1 Routeing slip 64; Manuals 65

10. Meetings   72
The meeting checklist 72; The agenda 74; The U-Drive Principle 74; Sample minutes 75; The minutes 76

11. The Curriculum Vitae and Letter of Application   77
The curriculum vitae 77; Sample CV 78; The covering letter 80; Sample covering letters 80; Exercise 11.1 CV and covering letter 82; Turning down a job offer 82; Exercise 11.2 Letter of refusal 82

Appendix   83
Exercise Answers 85

Further Reading from Kogan Page   104

Chapter 1
Introduction

What is defensive writing?

Most English courses stress problem solving, or what to do when you get into trouble. You may be having difficulty with spelling, grammar, sentence construction, or organisation.

This workbook is slightly different. It is based on the defensive driving approach to learning to drive a car. Like defensive driving, it will teach you to avoid problems by not getting into trouble.

The first rule of defensive driving is: you will be less likely to get into trouble if you are prepared for it. In other words, think ahead while driving, and be ready for situations which could cause accidents. Sometimes you can even take action before the danger appears, and avoid it entirely. The second rule of defensive driving is: if you are prepared for the worst, it won't happen.

For example, say you are going to use the word *ensure* in a sentence, such as:

This letter will ensure his acceptance.

You may not be sure whether the right word is *ensure* or *insure*. What do you do?

You can, of course, look up the words in a dictionary. This will take you about 60 seconds. Or you can use a shorter and easier method: don't use the word at all. Write:

This letter is sure to make him accept.

This is a simple way to solve the problem. More accurately, the problem hasn't been solved, it has been avoided. You can't be faced with a problem if you steer around it.

There are other problems in writing that can be avoided in much the same way. Long words, for example:

- are difficult to spell,
- can be mistyped,

- could be misused by the writer,
- could be misunderstood by the reader.

So, don't use them. Find a shorter word, or use two or three simple words to put across the meaning. Instead of saying *rehabilitate*, say *restore* or *return to normal*. Any word of more than four syllables is probably worth replacing in this way.

Some of the techniques for problem avoidance in this workbook are:

- limiting vocabulary,
- putting words nearest to their modifiers,
- making clauses shorter,
- using time flow as an organising tool in sentence and paragraph construction.

Who is this workbook for?

You've probably realised that this approach is a little different from the one you learned at school. What most people need is a writing guide that is simple to use. This guide should help you to produce memos, letters, reports, and other types of correspondence that all sorts of readers can easily understand. Complicated words and phrases will be avoided, standard ways of doing things will be given, and the process of putting ideas down on paper will be made as easy as possible.

This workbook will be of most help to:

(a) junior management, who are being asked for the first time to document events and write proposals,
(b) middle management, who find they need a faster, better, and clearer way of writing memos, letters, and reports,
(c) professionals whose first language is not English and who are being held back by their inability to write simple, clear English,
(d) anyone else who is not getting through to his or her readers.

Think of the time you will save: yours, mine, and that of all your other readers.

How to use this workbook

This workbook is divided into 11 chapters, each of which concentrates on certain aspects of your writing and gives you

Exercise 1.1

The defensive writing test

Before you get your driver's licence, you must pass a test. An instructor sits beside you and each time you make a mistake, he or she takes off points.

Let's take the same approach to something *you* have written, such as a memo or letter. Using the following checklist, mark yourself, and see how well you do. Use only one page of your writing. After you have completed the workbook, you might want to review this test and rewrite your memo using the defensive writing techniques you have learned.

Checklist

Points

1. For each word with more than three syllables, deduct *one* point for *each* syllable over three.
2. For each sentence of more than 20 words, deduct two points. If over 30 words, deduct four points.
3. For any sentence with more than four punctuation marks, deduct one point for each extra punctuation mark.
4. For each use of any of the following, deduct two points:
       ! ? " " ( ) —
5. For each sentence that does not have a subject, such as: *Mr Smith* or *I* or *the book*, deduct two points.
6. For each foreign word, take off two points.
7. For each Greek or Latin word or expression, such as *eg* or *ie*, take off one point.
8. For any paragraph of more than eight sentences, take off one point for each extra sentence.
9. For each change of tense in a sentence or a paragraph, take off two points.
10. Check each subject and verb for distance between them. For example, if you write:

    Our football team plays this Saturday

    this is good, as the verb *plays* follows directly after the subject *team*.

    For every word between subject and verb, take off one point. Do this for each sentence. If you can't find the verb in a sentence, take off five points.

Total score

techniques to make your writing shorter, simpler, and clearer.

Each chapter includes one or more exercises. In the exercises, you will be asked to apply what you have learned. You will find the answers and follow-up notes for the exercises in the Appendix.

Once basic writing skills are sharpened, memo, letter, and report writing will be covered. In each case, the simplest and easiest way of doing the job will be presented.

The purpose of this workbook is to encourage you to solve your own problems. What we learn by ourselves is learned best.

Let's begin with Exercise 1.1, the Defensive Writing Test, which will identify your major writing weaknesses and let you know how much you need this workbook.

If your score is five or less, perhaps you don't need this workbook. If your score is 75 or more, you should think of taking a basic or remedial English course. In between these two scores, this book will probably help you. Think of it in the same way as defensive driving courses given to drivers who have some experience, but who have developed dangerous driving habits. Defensive writing techniques will make your writing simpler, clearer, and less likely to create problems for your readers.

Chapter 2
Words

The purpose of this chapter is to teach you vocabulary reduction, which is the first and most important step in defensive writing. The longer the word you use, the more difficult it is to understand. Use short words and you are more likely to be understood.

This section will introduce you to many techniques which will simplify your vocabulary.

When you complete this chapter, you will

- know your skills as a defensive writer,
- reduce your writing vocabulary to its optimum size.

Vocabulary reduction

The average office dictionary has 30,000 to 40,000 words. Even a small pocket dictionary may have 25,000.

The average person knows about 5,000 words, but uses fewer than 3,000. Unfortunately, not everybody uses the same 3,000, so the standard vocabulary that everyone can understand is about 5,000 words. With a few exceptions, this is the English you hear on radio and television, and read in magazines such as *Reader's Digest*. There is nothing wrong with this limited vocabulary, and if you want to be understood by the greatest number of people, you should try to limit your vocabulary to these words.

As a general rule, don't use words that:

- are longer than four syllables,
- are foreign,
- start with *per, para,* and other Latin expressions,
- are highly technical,
- are hyphenated,
- have double letters, like *commemorate*.

1. The efficiency principle
Let's go back to Samuel Morse, who invented the Morse Code.

The idea of using dots and dashes to represent the letters of the alphabet was a good one, but Morse went one brilliant step further. Instead of making the letter *A* one dot, *B* a dot and a dash, and so on, Morse went into a printer's office. There he looked at the lead type used to print newspapers in order to determine which were the most common letters.

Morse found that *e* was the most common letter. He then assigned one dot to *e* and went looking for the next most common letter, *t*, which became one dash. The letter *a* was then represented by one dot followed by one dash, and so on.

In this way, Morse made his code very efficient. If you have a lot of *e*'s in your text and you use one dot per *e*, you will take far less time to send your message than a telegrapher using three dashes for each *e*. However, for a rare letter like *j*, you can afford a long code of one dot plus three dashes, as you will seldom be using it.

2. Techniques
How can this principle be applied to our writing? Here are some techniques:

(a) Don't use long words for simple things. Why say *adversary* when you can say *enemy*? If you must use *civilisation*, for example, use it seldom, and switch to words like *people* as often as you can. In fact, it is better to start with simple words like *people* and build up to complicated ones like *civilisation* as you go along. In this way, your reader will learn to understand the more difficult words.

(b) Don't try to express complicated thoughts with one word. Packing too much meaning into one word is like eating concentrated or very rich food. Your readers can get mental indigestion. As an example, take the word *capitalist*.

This is a favourite insult used by many of the world's socialist and communist parties. What it really means is a person who invests money in a business, in the hope of making money. The trouble with this word is that it can apply to a Rockefeller or to a corner-shop owner. In some parts of the world, it is applied to everyone, whether they own oil wells, sweet shops, or nothing.

How do you avoid using such words? Be specific instead of general. Say:

Exercise 2.1

Vocabulary reduction

Below you will find 20 words which are difficult to understand or spell. Replace them with the simplest and shortest equivalent word or group of words. If you like, use a *thesaurus*, for example *Roget's Thesaurus*, which is available as an inexpensive paperback, and gives lists of words that are similar in meaning.

1. Unconstrained
2. Obliterate
3. Systematic
4. Temperate
5. Circumspect
6. Indemnify
7. Indefensible
8. Flaccid
9. Exempt
10. Implicit
11. Explicit
12. Apparent
13. Eradicate
14. Erroneous
15. Itinerary
16. Equivocal
17. Perquisite
18. Paramount
19. Squeamish
20. Fallacy

Turn to the Appendix for the answers.

large investor

or *small investor*

or *sweet shop owner*

or *Rockefeller.*

To be fair, of course, you should avoid using the word *communist* to describe Eastern Europeans, other than the 10 per cent or so of the population who belong to a communist party.

As a general rule, the more complicated the idea, the more you should explain what you mean. Don't be afraid of using many words to describe a single idea, if you think you can be clearer.

(c) If you have some information to give, use as few words as possible if the information content is low. For example, how much information is in this sentence?

At precisely 5.05 am this morning, the sun rose in all its glory in the eastern part of the sky.

We all know the sun comes up early each morning, and

that it can't rise anywhere but in the sky and the east. So, the only information in these 20 words is the time of sunrise.

However, if the sun happens to rise in the west one day, *call attention to it* in any way you can. Do not slip it innocently into a sentence like the one above. Repeat the unusual fact at least twice, if you can, or underline it, or use capital letters. If the sun really came up in the west some day, your newspaper would run a long story about it. Use this principle as well when *you* have high information content. Give rare news a lot of coverage.

Conciseness

Most people's writing is like a garden filled with weeds, full of useless words that hide what the writer is trying to say. By weeding out words, or by using fewer words to say the same thing, your writing can be improved.

The next exercise will give you some useful practice in reducing the number of letters and words without removing information. You will not have to do much rewriting, just crossing out. For example, a sentence can be improved by doing this:

This is a subject which usually holds much interest for men.

Here we have crossed out seven words and changed *interest* to *interests*. You can rewrite it completely, of course:

Usually men are interested in this.

There is nothing wrong with this, but it takes much more time, and your time is valuable.

A word of caution about sentences 9, 10, and 11 in Exercise 2.2. In each of these we could replace whole groups of words with a single word which says exactly what we want. Unfortunately, these words are rare, and might not be understood by 99 per cent of your readers. So be careful, and don't confuse people by being too concise.

Say it more simply

Business writing is full of overused expressions that have crept in from the diplomatic, accounting, and legal professions. They

WORDS

Exercise 2.2

Shortening sentences (1)

Shorten and improve these sentences, without changing the original meaning.

1. If you want more modern equipment, you will have to go to a manufacturer that is larger in size.
2. Without these important qualities, you will be nothing but a failure as far as being a manager goes.
3. The nature of the calculations needed to arrive at a good office design is outlined on page 60.
4. The two lists came to a total sum of £479.
5. Please bring this file to a hasty conclusion.
6. The car's engine was running at a high rate of speed.
7. On the date of 4 June we shall begin plant operations.
8. This recommendation is found to be preferable by myself.
9. The excavation hole depth was great.
10. We saw a large number of people working at their desks.
11. The majority of serious accidents have occurred during times when traffic activity was at a peak.
12. Any of the building plots will be dimensionally capable of accommodating house design number 31.
13. Acorn Industries has made many organisational changes needed to be made in order for it to become a better company.
14. In accordance with your request, attached please find our financial statement giving sales volume prior to the date of 12 February 1985.

Correct answers are in the Appendix.

give your correspondence an old-fashioned and formal sound that can annoy a reader. These expressions are mostly meaningless or vague.

Don't say, for example, 'at an early date', when you can say, 'before 15 July, 198-'. The first phrase allows the *reader* to decide when to act. The second gives him or her a deadline. If you want your reader to do something by a certain date, say so.

Read the following list of expressions, and remember, as a general rule, not to use them in your next business letter or memo.

above
are in receipt of
as a matter of fact
as per
as to
at an early date
at this point in time
at this writing
at which time
at your earliest convenience
attached please
come to light
condition
consideration
consideration with regard to
definite
degree
finalise
from the point of view of
hereby
herein
hereinafter
hereto
herewith
I remain
inasmuch as
in actual fact
in connection with
in reference to
in regard to
in relation to
insofar as
in that
in the region of
in this instance

in the majority of instances
in the position
it is our (my) opinion that
it is recommended that
kindly
permit me to say
please find enclosed
position previous to
prioritise
pursuant to your request
recent date
referring to your request
situation (this situation)
take this opportunity
thanking you in advance
the fact that
the facts of the matter are
the situation in regard to
there is evidence that
thereof
this matter
to the extent that
to the point where
trusting you will
under separate cover
we hope; we trust
wherein
wish to
with a need to
with regard to
with respect to
would like to
your case
your experience

Exercise 2.3

Shortening sentences (2)

1. All these events should be listed in the consecutive order in which they occurred.
2. Switzerland is another winter sports country that attracts visitors.
3. All the tins were closed, so that the air could not touch the contents.
4. Cornflour is a food that can be easily dissolved in liquid.
5. This insect is so small that it is seen only by looking through a microscope.
6. The road sign was located at the place where the two roads intersected.
7. We should thoroughly discuss the question as to whether we should leave today.
8. Dogs are animals that can eat every type of food.
9. Petrol is a liquid that can or will be easily ignited.
10. The fact that we have received our diplomas indicates progress.
11. My next-door neighbours, who came from Italy, are applying for their naturalisation papers tomorrow.
12. The place for which the boat was headed was kept secret from us.
13. Now there is a meeting going on in Suite 200.
14. Instead of stopping, the taxi driver made the cab go faster.
15. The story told by the lawyer was impossible to believe.
16. She was possessed by a desire to achieve a high station in life.
17. The floors were too cold for comfort in many cases.
18. Using a computer keyboard, you should exercise a light touch on the keys.
19. The computer, which was unheard of as late as the 1940s, has changed the face of business activities.
20. It is extremely rare that a mistake is made in counting the church collection.

Correct answers are in the Appendix

THE BUSINESS WRITING WORKBOOK

Exercise 2.4

Reducing standard phrases

These are all standard phrases in business letters that are long-winded ways of saying something very simple. Say the same thing in fewer words. If you think the phrase can be left out completely, write *omit*.

1. In the normal course of our procedures
2. We have discontinued the policy of
3. Therefore we ask that you remit
4. Will you please arrange to send
5. We are of the opinion that
6. In view of the fact that
7. Will you be good enough to
8. At all times
9. In regard to
10. In the near future
11. In view of the above
12. In the amount of £100.49
13. Under date of 6 June
14. The facts of the matter are
15. In the event that
16. At the present time
17. In advance of
18. Come to a decision
19. Grant approval
20. Come to an end
21. Owing to the fact that
22. Make a revision
23. I was unaware of the fact that
24. In spite of the fact that
25. He is a man who
26. As soon as possible

Correct answers are in the Appendix.

Chapter 3
Phrases and Punctuation

The purpose of this chapter is to teach you how to write and organise your phrases. You will learn how to cut out useless phrases, correct dangling phrases, and simplify punctuation. In this way, your phrases will be clearer and more effective.

When you complete this chapter, you will

- understand how to recognise and remove useless phrases,
- understand what punctuation is really for and how to avoid many punctuation marks.

Dangling phrases

If we want to show that two things are linked, we generally put them as close to each other in a sentence as we can. But sometimes, closely related facts get separated in the act of writing. Let's look at some horrible examples.

> *No one is allowed to dump anything beside this road except the refuse collector.*

Here the phrase *except the refuse collector* modifies, or changes the phrase *No one*.

But these two ideas are at opposite ends of the sentence. This makes it difficult to see that they are closely linked, and the sentence is unclear.

It should read:

> *No one except the refuse collector is allowed to dump anything beside this road.*

We saw that the problem in the original sentence was the distance between the phrase *No one* and the modifier *except the refuse collector*.

This is called a *dangling modifier* and many variations of it exist. Here's another.

> *Swimming across the bay, a shark surprised him.*

In grammar books, this is called the dangling (or hanging) participle error. *Swimming* is the present participle of the verb *to swim*, and it is dangling because it is not attached to anything in the sentence. In fact, the *man* is swimming. This sentence should read:

> *While he was swimming across the bay, a shark surprised him.*

A good rule is never to start a sentence with a phrase like *Swimming across the bay . . .*

Another good rule is to put closely related words as close together as you can. Best of all, have them side by side. In this way your reader will know they are closely related.

Exercise 3.1

Dangling phrases

Correct these sentences by putting closely related phrases more closely together. Make other changes where necessary.

1. After talking to my accountant, my bank balance improved.
2. Julia's child fell out of the tree in her lunch hour, and was rushed to the hospital by the school nurse with a possible fractured arm.
3. Walking down Hastings Street, the new hotel towers above the other buildings.
4. Driving recklessly, the police officer arrested the driver.
5. After soaking in the alcohol for a day, I prepared the specimen for the lab.
6. As an employee in our company, these forms will be useful to you.
7. Egypt's administration under Mubarak, now six years old, has done much to advance the cause of peace in the Arab world.
8. Wayne Gretsky received another award for scoring after the game.

Correct answers are in the Appendix.

Punctuation Guide

Here are the most common punctuation marks:

.	*full stop*	—	*dash*
,	*comma*	-	*hyphen*
;	*semicolon*	'	*apostrophe*
:	*colon*	" "	*double quotation marks*
?	*question mark*	' '	*single quotation marks*
!	*exclamation mark*	( )	*parentheses (sometimes called brackets)*

They can be put into three groups:

(a) Marks that divide or end sentences.
(b) Marks that show emotion.
(c) Marks that indicate conversation.

If you think about it, it would be very difficult to read a story aloud without these marks. How would you know when to end a sentence, or express surprise, or hesitate in the middle of a sentence? Perhaps punctuation was invented to allow us to imitate speech in our writing.

1. Pauses

Someone giving a speech has to stop every few seconds or run out of breath. The speechmaker puts his or her ideas together in sentences and stops at the end of each sentence. In writing, we use a full stop to show this. To show a short pause, we use a comma. A longer pause might call for a semicolon or colon.

Let's put these pauses in order of length, with increasing length from left to right.

> , ; : .

Read aloud a sentence you have just written, and you will have little trouble deciding what punctuation to use. If you sometimes have trouble choosing between the comma and the semicolon, use the comma. Use the colon only before lists of three or more items.

2. The apostrophe

> '

The apostrophe causes a lot of trouble. It has three uses, but it can often be avoided.

(a) It can show the leaving out of a letter or letters, as in *can't* for *cannot*. Of course, you can write out the word and not worry about the apostrophe. This will make your writing sound formal and precise, which is fine in reports.
(b) The apostrophe can be used to show possession, as in

somebody else's child

Try to avoid this construction. You can say

the child of somebody else.

You can omit the apostrophe and your meaning will still be clear, but you may be criticised. However, you will be writing more easily, and you will be understood.
(c) An apostrophe and the letter *s* is sometimes used to show the plurals of letters, numerals and words.

Don't use and's and but's too often.
My father was in Europe in the 1950's.

You can eliminate the apostrophe and still be perfectly well understood.

We now come to the most common mistake in English. *It's* is short for *it is* or *it has* and *its* is a word which shows possession, as in

its own home

Before you write *its*, think whether you mean *it is* or *it has*, and if you do, write it out as *it is* (or *it has*).

Otherwise, write *its*. Remember, avoid apostrophes.

3. Other punctuation marks

(a) The exclamation mark

!

Never use the exclamation mark in business or technical writing. It can have strong emotional content, and emotion has no place in this type of writing.

(b) The question mark

?

Avoid the question mark. Questions are a good teaching device, but in correspondence you should not be teaching. Questions can also sound as if you are putting your reader on the spot.

(c) Dash

$$-$$

Many people use the dash as a universal punctuation mark. It can sound as if your thoughts are somehow disconnected from each other. You don't want to sound this way, so instead of the dash, use a comma.

(d) The hyphen

$$-$$

The hyphen is shorter than the dash, and many people confuse the two. It is supposed to be used between parts of a word to make up a new or compound word. Use it as little as possible. There are very few in this book.

(e) Quotation marks

$$"\,"\\ '\,'$$

Double and single quotation marks are also difficult. In most business and technical correspondence, you rarely have to quote anyone. If you do, say something along the lines of

Jones said he would do it tomorrow

This does not sound like Jones talking, but it gets the meaning across just as well.

(f) Parentheses (or brackets)

$$(\ )$$

Parentheses are used to enclose less important explanations in a sentence, much as you would say 'by the way' in conversation. They have little place in writing that has to be direct and forceful. Don't use them unless you have to.

We have now gone from 12 punctuation marks to four. You or your secretary will be pleased, as punctuation slows down any typing job. However, the main improvement is that you will rid yourself of worrying about some unimportant writing details. More important still, your writing will be clearer.

Exercise 3.2

Punctuation

Punctuate and capitalise the following letter. Correct spelling errors. Use only essential punctuation.

8 april 1987

mr john w smith
general manager
intercontinental services ltd
2055 main road
westview wiltshire

dear mr smith

thank you for your letter of 6 march which we have just received it must have been delayed by the mail strike

the conference has been rescheduled for the weekend of may 23 24 inclusive it will be held at the landmark hotel 25 robert street our guest of honour ms shirley jones will deliver a major speach at 8 pm on friday the 22nd her topic will be women in advertising the delegates will also hear panels on the following topics current problems in advertising the challenge of consumerism and new marketing trends it promises to be a lively and interesting meeting if you still wish to attend please send your check for £25 to cover registration fees and add £10 if you wish to attend the banquet saturday night gratuity included we look forword to seeing you please accept my apologies for the delay in answerring your letter.

yours sincerely
thomas a weston
information director
advertising council

Correct answers are in the Appendix.

Chapter 4
Sentences and Paragraphs

The purpose of this chapter is to provide some useful ways to make your sentences shorter, clearer, and more effective. Most sentences are more complicated than the thoughts they express. Such sentences can be improved by better subject and verb agreement, more parallel structure, and reduction in length and punctuation.

You will also learn to do a better job of organising your thoughts. You will be introduced to some techniques that will help you group sentences into paragraphs that have a logical structure.

When you complete this chapter, you will

- have two useful rules for reducing sentence length and punctuation,
- understand how to make your writing more forceful by avoiding writing 'backwards' or in the passive voice,
- understand how parallel structure in a sentence can express your thoughts more clearly and forcefully,
- know how to avoid subject and verb agreement problems,
- understand and use the 'time line' in paragraphs.

Sentences

1. Reducing sentence length and punctuation

Rule 1: No sentence should be more than 20 words long.

Rule 2: No sentence should have more than four punctuation marks

The human brain can only absorb a certain amount of written information at a time. If the sentence is too long, the brain rejects the information, or loses track of it. Here is a horrible example:

> *When I think back on my early life, or at least, that part of it that could be called early childhood, I can see, now, that Aunt Eleanor was not, nor had she ever been, one of those people who could be considerate of a small child's tender, easily bruised feelings.*

What's wrong with this sentence?

Fifty-one words are too much to digest. There are also eight commas, which chop the sentence up into many small pieces. Because this is one sentence, our minds expect it to be about one thing or subject. At the same time, the mind has to take each piece of information and sort it into some logical pattern. When a sentence is too long, or too chopped up, or both, we get confused. Let's rewrite it.

> *When I was a child, Aunt Eleanor hurt my feelings.*

This, of course, is a less literary sentence, but the meaning is the same. It is also much clearer.

Remember our two rules: you should not use more than 20 words and four punctuation marks. You can, of course, sometimes break these rules, but if you stick to them as much as possible, many of your sentences will be easier to understand.

2. Introducing logical sequence in sentences

With a little forethought, you can write sentences that follow a logical sequence, like this:

First clause: *Background*, or explanation, of earliest events
Example:

> *When I was a little boy,*

Second clause: *Events*, or what happened next
Example:

> *I had severe arthritis,*

Third clause: *Results*, or the conclusion
Example:

> *which ever since has made it difficult for me to walk.*

Here the clauses are separated by commas. As usual, each comma indicates a short pause, but more important, each clause describes a different time frame. These frames are like photos of an event. First we see the boy. Then we see him with arthritis, and last we see him as grown up. The events occurred in this order and the sentence follows this pattern. You can produce many other versions of this sentence by changing the sequence of events.

For example:

> *I have found it difficult to walk ever since I had severe arthritis as a child.*

There is nothing really wrong with this. It tells you something and then gives you the reason, which is a common way of saying things. The mind, however, has to move back in time, which is a less logical sequence than the one given in the first example.

A smooth flow of events should appear on the page, and the brain should be fed these events in the order that they actually happened. If you learn to do this with sentences, then you will find it easier when we begin to work on mastering the paragraph and improving overall composition skills.

3. Writing backwards

> *This puzzle could only be solved by him.*

In grammar books this is called the *passive voice*, but we can think of it as simply 'writing backwards'. The active version of this is

> *Only he could solve this puzzle.*

This is a far better way of putting down the facts. It is shorter, simpler, and stronger English. The passive voice version sounds confusing and weak by comparison. Avoid writing backwards if you can, even if for some reason you want to sound formal. Don't say:

> *This drink is enjoyed by many Americans.*

Say

> *Many Americans enjoy this drink.*

Notice how much more natural this last sentence sounds. We are used to sentences that follow natural sequences.

Take a cricket player in action:

- We see the player standing by the wicket.
- The bat moves and we hear the crack as it hits the ball.
- We see the ball on its way to the outfield.

Exercise 4.1

Eliminating the passive voice

Below are 10 examples of writing in the passive voice. Turn these sentences around, and make them shorter, simpler, and stronger.

1. None of the above was understood by anyone.

2. The undersigned was not contacted by your office.

3. It has frequently been suggested by our company that your expenses are tax deductible.

4. This programme has been neglected by many of our viewers, who have been annoyed by its contents.

5. In certain circumstances, we have been asked by our customers to give discounts.

6. May we suggest that we not be asked to consider these alternatives at this time.

7. This government has been asked by its many critics to cancel its aid to this nation.

8. I have been approached by many of our creditors to relax our penalty charges.

9. When two interest payments have been applied and not met, often the payment schedule has been abandoned.

10. The computer has not been received with much favour in some industries.

To describe these three events in their normal and logical order, why not use this same order in our sentence?

He hit the ball has:

(a) subject *(He)*,
(b) a verb *(hit)*,
(c) an object *(ball)*.

This is the best and clearest kind of sentence, and you should try to imitate it as much as you can.

4. Using parallel structure

Many examples of bad writing have poor *parallel structure*. What does this expression mean?

We see something *parallel* as being lined up with something else. There is a certain harmony in the arrangement that pleases us. In a similar way, we can write down groups of thought that are parallel, or going in the same direction. Here is an example:

The applicant is young and seems to be capable, with an attractive appearance.

Here the writer is describing the applicant, and has noted three things he or she likes. The applicant is:

- young
- capable
- attractive.

The writer has, however, used three different ways of putting these ideas across. Let's compare them by putting them in column form.

- is young
- seems to be capable
- with an attractive appearance.

You can see that the first two phrases have verbs, while the third doesn't. The first two phrases also end with adjectives, while the third ends with a noun. The second phrase is also different in form from the first phrase, because the words *to be* follow the verb.

We have three closely related ideas here that are each expressed in a different way, which takes away from their closeness. Why not say:

The applicant is young, capable, and attractive.

Exercise 4.2

Parallel structure

Rewrite these sentences, and use parallel structure to make them clearer.

1. Mr Johns is a man of integrity who has a good track record of achievement.
2. I told Steve that he should spend more of his time on work and stop visiting around the building.
3. The manual is out of stock and not being reprinted.
4. He said that he would return soon and for all of us to work hard while he was away.
5. In the civil engineering course every student learns the use of a theodolite and how to survey the property.
6. Jack's job is promoting computers and to sell a good image of the company.
7. The salesman's presentation was too long, boring, and could not be heard beyond the middle of the auditorium.
8. I like looking at a game of football on TV, and also to watch soap operas.
9. Our library is a good place for researchers, and you can do some casual reading there, also.
10. Jack asked me to stop at the supermarket and also wanted me to visit the pet shop on my way home.

Correct answers are in the Appendix.

You might argue that this changes the meaning slightly, as the writer originally said *seems to be capable*.

But if your impression of someone is that they are capable, you may as well say they are. It is only an opinion, and your readers will accept it as that. Don't be afraid to change the meaning slightly to achieve a parallel structure and a better effect. If you are writing business documents, such as memos, reports, and letters, you want your readers to *do* what you suggest. Parallel structure can be very effective.

Notice how much stronger the sentence is after we put it into parallel form. In fact, it sounds like part of a speech, and good speakers use this technique as often as they can.

For effect, you can sometimes repeat words to force ideas into parallel forms. A little of this in a memo is enough, however.

5. Avoiding subject and verb agreement problems

Every few weeks I listen to a news broadcast relayed from a small village called Old Crow in the northern tip of the Yukon. The reporter is Edith Josie, and she does a wonderful job of describing the life of this remote community. Her first line is always: *Here are the news.* When I first heard this, I smiled. Then I started thinking that maybe she was right, and that the word *news* should be plural.

The problem of subject and verb arrangement, as it is called in grammar books, is one all of us have to face from time to time. But by using defensive writing techniques, we can avoid subject and verb agreement problems. Here are some suggestions:

(a) Don't say:

> *Each eligible man and woman has/have been contacted by the social worker.*

Say:

> *The social worker has contacted each eligible man and woman.*

Often, if you turn the sentence around, you can avoid the problem.

(b) Don't say:

> *A series of workshops was held.*

Say:

> *Four workshops were held.*

Many nouns such as:

> *group   pair   committee   couple*

sound plural, but are singular. Worse, these nouns are vague. If you know how many people there were, why not say so?

(c) Avoid constructions such as:

> *None of*
> *Some of*
> *All of*
> *Half of*
> *Which of*

THE BUSINESS WRITING WORKBOOK

> **Exercise 4.3**
>
> **Subject and verb agreement**
>
> Here are some sentences which may make you wonder if the verb agrees with the subject. Rewrite them to avoid any problems.
>
> 1. Five pounds are missing.
> 2. The committee have not wanted to change for personal expenses.
> 3. It seems that he or I have to do all the work.
> 4. Neither of the candidates show promise.
> 5. The jury have selected their hotel rooms.
> 6. The couple at the head table are called Peters.
> 7. Some of our fees has been spent.
> 8. Either of the twins are going with us.
> 9. Pulling and pushing is the hard part.
> 10. On the field stands a man and a woman.
>
> Correct answers are in the Appendix.

- Use *no one* for *none* if you can.
- Don't use *some of*, as this is vague.
- Why say *all of my staff* when you can simply say *my staff*?
- Use the exact number instead of *half of*.

There are other good reasons for avoiding these constructions. Take this sentence:

None of the people were wrong.

Some grammar books will tell you this is incorrect. *None* is short for *no one* and the sentence should be:

None of the people was wrong.

But this sounds terrible, doesn't it? Part of the problem is that the subject *none* is too far away from its verb *was wrong*. If you keep subject and verb side by side, problems tend to go away. Look at the above sentence again. How about this version?

No one was wrong.

This is short, simple and easy. Why not do it this way?

Exercise 4.4

The time line (1)

Here is a newspaper story that, in keeping with good journalistic practice, is not strictly organised in time sequence. As an exercise, rewrite it in the order in which the events occurred. Leave the first two paragraphs alone, as they are a good summary of the story.

An easy way to rewrite this is to isolate the facts and number them in sequence. You could do this by choosing the first event that happened and putting a *1* against it on your copy of the story. The first fact is that Zurfluh's vehicle was seen weaving down the motorway. The next event is his running from his vehicle, so number that *2*. Keep going.

Once you have all the facts in sequence, rewriting is fairly straightforward. You may like the original better, but this is such a good story that almost any version would be equally funny.

Notice the headline. The reporter used the words 'feast fails', though in fact Zurfluh's actions were *wasted*, and not a failure. This is good journalism, but you should make sure your paragraph headings are accurate.

Turn to the Appendix for a rewritten version.

UNDERSHORTS FEAST FAILS*

STETTLER, Alta (CP) — David Zurfluh tried to eat his undershorts on the theory the cotton fabric might absorb the alcohol in his stomach before he underwent a breathalyser test.

He found out Thursday it was a wasted effort.

The 18-year-old from Stettler appeared in provincial court and was acquitted on a charge of impaired driving because the breath analysis showed his blood alcohol level exactly at the legal limit of .08 milligrams per 100 millilitres.

Zurfluh was collared by Pc Bill Robinson after he ran from his vehicle, which had been seen weaving down the motorway, and was put into a patrol car.

Zurfluh told Judge David MacNaughton he ripped the crotch out of his shorts as he sat in the car, stuffed the fabric in his mouth and then spat it out.

Students from a local school, in court to view the workings of the law, had difficulty maintaining their composure when the testimony grew lively and were removed by their teacher.

'People were leaving the courtroom with tears in their eyes', said Constable Peter MacFarlane.

* Reprinted by permission of *The Canadian Press*

THE BUSINESS WRITING WORKBOOK

Exercise 4.5

The time line (2)

Suppose your manager has asked you to write up a proposal for converting your manual office correspondence system to a new word processor which he or she has selected.

You assemble some facts, in point form, that look like this:

- Accounting procedures will have to be changed so that they will be compatible with the new filing system.
- The board of directors will have to approve £20,000 for the machine.
- Sales brochures should be revised to show that this service is available to customers.
- Office staff will need retraining.

Number these points in the sequence in which they will occur, and put them into a paragraph. Write a good sentence that sums up the proposal, and put it at the beginning or end of your paragraph.

Turn to the Appendix for a suggested paragraph.

Paragraphs

The time line is a simple method of organising your writing. It works well in sentences, memos, letters, and reports as well as in paragraphs. It is not the only way to organise writing, but it is the simplest. You probably remember that in sentence construction I suggested that you write facts in the order in which they actually happened. Let me now put it more strongly:

Write down events in the order that they happened.

In other words, if A happened before B, write down A and then B. This sounds simpler than it is. Many people like to write backwards in time, and some bounce back and forth between past and future, even in the same sentence.

A good teacher will start a lesson by describing the main principles or ideas to be learned by the students. The teacher then outlines all the reasons or methods that support these principles. At the end of the lesson, the teacher ties all the details together and restates the principles.

You can do this in your writing as well. The first sentence in a paragraph should be a summary of what you are trying to do in the paragraph. For example, if the first paragraph is *background* material, say so in the first sentence. Another way of doing this is to use headings. If you use the heading *Background* at the start of a paragraph, your reader will know what is coming, and will be more likely to follow what you are trying to say.

Chapter 5
Memos

The purpose of this chapter is to teach you some techniques that will make your memos more effective. You must have a goal in writing a memo, and you must make every effort to see that this goal results in some positive action by your reader.

When you complete this chapter you will

- have a checklist to help you determine the purpose and tone of your memos,
- know the standard memo format,
- be familiar with the four steps in writing a memo.

Memo checklist

Think before you write a memo to someone. A piece of paper has many sharp edges and I've known many readers and writers who have been cut. You can say things over the phone and upset people, but saying it on paper may make them really angry.

Over the years I've made a lot of mistakes. Each time I've realised this, I have added another item to my memo checklist. The list is still growing and here it is. Notice that many of these are designed to keep you out of trouble. This is what defensive writing is all about.

1. Should this be a memo? Why not make a phone call, or a personal visit?
2. Are you writing to the right person?
3. Are you bypassing anyone in the process?
4. To whom should you send information copies?
5. Are you asking for information, telling someone to do something, or merely passing on information? Are you clear on the purpose of this memo?
6. If you are requesting action, are you doing it politely?
7. Is there any emotional content? If so, remove it.
8. Are there any phrases or expressions which you think

are particularly good or clever? Strike them out.
9. If you want something, have you said by what date?
10. Have you checked the memo against the office standard for the correct format?
11. If possible, put the memo aside until the next day to see if it still sounds good.
12. If you have any doubts about anything in it, don't send it. Your intuition is probably right.
13. If the memo is more than one typewritten page it probably won't be read carefully, if at all. Shorten it.
14. Try to put yourself in the reader's shoes. Would the memo be clear to you?
15. What will happen after your memo is read? Are you prepared for the reaction?
16. Can you avoid receiving a reply in the form of another memo? Do you want to generate another piece of paper?

If you want to close the file on this subject, think about what replies you may receive, and stop them from happening. See the section on the Zero Reply Principle in Chapter 6 for more tips.

Most of these points apply to letters as well. Read the checklist before and after writing a letter.

The standard memo format

1. Subject
Try to paraphrase the whole idea of the memo. For example:
> *Promotion of Ms Smith to Group 10.*

2. Reference
Refer to any previous correspondence that deals specifically with the subject matter. One reference is usually enough. For example:
> *Memo, Smith to Jones, dated 11 February 198-, file 8-01; subject, Promotion Policy.*

3. Text
The text should follow a time line and describe the past, present, and future. This is a useful and effective way of grouping thoughts to form your paragraphs, and it also keeps your paragraphs in a logical sequence.

(a) First paragraph(s) — *Background*
    This most important section brings the reader up to date.

Exercise 5.1

Short memo

Write a memo to your boss, Peter Jones, based on the following information:

(a) A week ago he sent you a note asking you to investigate a problem with a power supply. The output fuses were blowing several times a day.
(b) You investigated and found that the load was the problem. Apparently, the current required from the power supply was too large when the load was first plugged in.
(c) You tried putting in larger fuses, but the power supply became damaged when the load was connected. You fixed the damage.
(d) You can't think of any solution, except buying a larger power supply.

Use the following memo form.

Memo to: Date:
From: File:
Subject:
Reference:

                                            (Sign at bottom)

For a sample memo, turn to the Appendix.

It says why a problem exists. If you omit this background, your reader may not understand the problem, or its importance.

(b) Second paragraph(s) — *Investigation*
This should state in some logical sequence the way in which the problem was investigated. Be brief.
(c) Third paragraph(s) — *Recommendations and Conclusions*
Make your recommendations and follow up with what may happen if they are accepted.

Exercise 5.2

Memo report

A background memo report is often required before an organisation will take action, and approval may be needed by a number of people. The next exercise is typical.

The memo has to have all the important facts. It will have to convince quite a few people. You should therefore write this memo anticipating that what you have written will be passed up to management. If your memo is good it will go up the organisational ladder without coming back to you for re-writing or explanation.

Include the following information in your memo:

(a) You are a Personnel Assistant in a large insurance company.

(b) The General Manager receives a letter from Mrs P J Jones, the widow of one of your ex-managers. She needs to go into hospital for a serious operation and had applied to the private medical scheme to which her bushand had contributed during his working life, to know what her rights are and what contribution she can expect towards her medical expenses.

   She found, to her distress, that when her husband died, in the service of the company, his contribution ceased and that, contrary to her belief, she, as his widow, could not draw on their scheme. She would welcome an explanation.

(c) You check Mr Jones's record with the company and find that he retired some months before his official retirement date, which was 1 August, his sixtieth birthday. Although the matter was never made public, he was asked to leave early because of the irreconcilable differences between himself and the director to whom he was responsible on the question of reorganising the department. His intransigent attitude was apparent to the staff, causing efficiency to suffer and, as a result, staffing costs rose and business was lost. The matter came to a crisis when he deliberately tipped hot coffee in the computer and he was only saved from instant dismissal by his excellent previous record.

(d) You have to write a memo report, explaining this situation.

For examples of memos you might write, turn to the Appendix.

Steps in memo writing

(a) Read the checklist on pages 36-7.
(b) Make an outline. Decide first what general topics will be in your main paragraphs, and then write down all the facts and thoughts you have that you will put into

these paragraphs. Number these in a logical sequence.
(c) Write the memo in double-spaced draft form. Make sure you have included all the facts. Put the memo aside until the next day.
(d) Re-read the checklist, then re-read your draft memo. Take out all unnecessary facts and words. Prepare final copy of memo.

Chapter 6
Letters

The purpose of this chapter is to give you some useful ways to make your letters reach the right person in the right way. Letters are important documents with possible legal or financial consequences. They deserve careful attention.

When you complete this chapter, you will

(a) know the zero reply principle,
(b) have guidelines on when to use *we* or *I*, and
(c) know how to write letters of rejection.

The zero reply principle

A letter can be written in many ways. Before you write it, you should consider what options you have, and what you want to do. Let's take the situation involving Mrs Jones in the previous chapter as an example. Suppose a course of action is approved and you are asked to draft a letter to her.

Letters are expensive to write, type, post and file. One of your objectives should be to reduce costs, so your letter should be short. What you must do, however, is reply to Mrs Jones in such a way that you never hear from her again. This is the zero reply principle.

How can you do this? Here is a checklist of do's and don'ts that apply to letters like these.

(a) *Don't* ask questions unless you have to. For example, don't ask Mrs Jones if she wants to rejoin the medical scheme at her own expense.
(b) *Don't* raise new points. For example, Mrs Jones said nothing about pension benefits, so don't mention them to her. If you do, you may receive a letter from her opening up a whole new problem area.
(c) *Do* be diplomatic, or tactful, or friendly, or whatever the situation calls for. For example, saying 'no' to Mrs Jones without being tactful and without saying why, is wrong.

It is not only bad manners, but also poor writing. It will make her angry; she will write another letter, and you will have to send her another reply.

(d) *Don't* admit error unless you have to.

(e) Once it is clear that you are wrong, however, *don't* be shy about admitting your mistake. Say 'I was wrong'. Don't cover up this statement with a lot of words. You may confuse the issue and invite a reply.

(f) *Do* think of the person receiving your letter. What will he or she do next? Will you receive a reply asking for more information? Then include it. Will you be asked to prepare some document? Then prepare the document in advance and attach it to your letter. In this way you will not receive a reply.

(g) *Don't* be vague. If you have a reason for something, give it. If you have to say something, say it without frills.

Exercise 6.1

Letter

In Chapter 5 you wrote a memo report about Mr Jones. Now assume that your report is approved and you are asked to write a letter to Mrs Jones, to be signed by the head of your department. You are to tell Mrs Jones what the company is prepared to do for her.

For a sample letter to Mrs Jones, turn to the Appendix.

We and I

Many of us have trouble with these two pronouns. When should you use *we* or *I* in a sentence to a customer, for example? Let's invent another test you can use to find out whether *we* or *I* is correct.

Suppose you are driving a car with your son or daughter. You hear a siren, see a flashing light, and an officer pulls you over. As you roll down the window, he asks, 'How fast were you going?'

You have two choices of pronoun. You can say, 'I was doing about 30' or, 'We were doing about 30'. Both answers are correct, but the second sounds as if you are sharing the blame or responsibility for what you are doing. *You* were driving, not your son or daughter, and though all of you were travelling at the same speed, you will get the ticket.

This is our old friend, the driver's seat test. If *you* are responsible or will be held responsible for what has happened, you should say *I*.

Let's look at some more examples. Suppose you are answering a complaint letter from a customer, who is unhappy about one of the products your company has made. You did not personally make the item, but must send the customer a replacement. In this case you represent the company and can take the blame by saying:

> *We are extremely sorry that our disk drive has not performed correctly. Please return it and we will send another.*

You could in fact say *I* for *we* in this sentence and still keep *our disk drive*. No one would expect you to be responsible for a faulty item produced by a large factory, but they might appreciate the personal touch put across by the use of *I*.

Let's go back to the driver's seat test. If you were *not* driving when the officer pulled the car over, and he asks how fast the car was going, suppose you leaned over the driver and said, 'We were only doing 30.'

What would the officer's reaction be? First, he asked the driver, not you. Second, the driver is responsible for what the car is doing, not the passenger.

Out of all this we can write three rules to help decide when to use *we* or *I*:

(a) If you did or thought something, say *I*.
(b) If you were responsible for what someone else did, say *we*.
(c) If neither of these fits, don't use any personal pronoun.

The third rule needs a little explanation. Complete this sentence:

> *do not believe your estimate is accurate.*

Sometimes you have to tell someone, in language that can't be misunderstood, that he or she is wrong. Would you start the above sentence with *we* or *I*?

It's tempting to hide behind *we*, but your reader will know you're hiding and be annoyed. There also isn't any point in using the word *I*, as this sounds too personal. You don't want your reader to think you are out to get him or her. Why not say:

> *Your estimate is not accurate, because . . .*

This is businesslike and factual, rather than personal and vague. Remember that the word *believe* in the first example implies that you don't really know what you're saying.

Exercise 6.2

Rejection letter

Assume that you are the personnel officer in a medium-sized insurance company. You have advertised for a Marketing Manager in the local newspaper and received over a hundred cvs. After some weeding, you have decided to bring in ten applicants for *interview*.

You must now write letters to *all the other* applicants, thanking them, and telling them that they are not being considered for the job. We are talking about over 90 letters, so you must come up with a standard response that will be a form letter, with a different name and address on each letter. This will disappoint almost a hundred people, and your job will be to make sure that these people will not be upset with you or your company.

Write the letter.

Turn to the Appendix for a suggested rejection letter.

Rejection letters

Let's say that you are taking on someone for an important job, perhaps one directly under you. You narrow the field down to three or four candidates, pick one, and then send an offer. What do you do about the others?

If you have a personnel department, the temptation is to let them do the dirty work of telling the other applicants. But if you interviewed these people, I think you owe them a personal letter. This is not only good manners but good business. Suppose the person you chose doesn't show up? You will then have to select another one of the candidates, and you want to be on good terms with him or her.

Here are some ideas you can use for rejection letters:

(a) Praise the person's abilities or experience where at all possible. Say that the applicant impressed you in a certain area, or that he or she was outstanding in some respect, if you can. Be specific or it will sound like a form letter.

(b) If you think the applicant could improve in some way, why not suggest it? Don't say he or she was rejected because of some personal characteristics. If more education, or training, or experience of a certain kind is needed, it is perfectly acceptable for you to say so. The applicant may even thank you some day for the good advice. At least you have tried to be not only friendly, but helpful. And if you can steer the candidate into another job opening, he or she will be grateful.

Chapter 7
Reports

This chapter is designed to help you write better formal reports. Many memos, including those you have done in previous chapters, are reports. A formal report, however, is a much larger and more complicated document. In this chapter, we will go into its structure in detail.

When you complete this chapter, you will

- know the parts of a formal report,
- be able to organise the parts effectively,
- have some useful guidelines on report presentation.

Parts of a formal report

The following nine parts of a formal report are described in the order in which they should appear in your report.

1. Cover
This should be a tough jacket that will survive hundreds of readings. You should print only the report title on it. If you use a clear or tinted plastic cover, you will not have to print the cover, as your reader will see the title page through the plastic.

2. Title page
As mentioned above, the title page can do double duty as the cover and should have:

   (a) a title,
   (b) the name of the receiver of the report, if needed,
   (c) the author's name, and organisation, if needed,
   (d) the date issued,
   (e) distribution and confidentiality, and
   (f) the file or report number.

3. Summary
It is probably only necessary for a long report. Write it last,

after you have written the whole report and put it after the title page. Campbell's Soup finds it easier to condense a soup after making it; in the same way, a summary is a boiling down of the whole report after you have written it.

It should explain:

(a) why the report was written,
(b) why the investigation was done,
(c) what the major findings, conclusions, or recommendations were.

The summary should take up no more than 12 typed lines, and should be designed for *information retrieval.* That is, the summary should be full of *key words* that can be put into a computer. For example, say your report deals with:

(a) accounting procedures,
(b) western banks,
(c) debentures,
(d) inflation.

Be sure to have all these key phrases in your summary. In this way, a librarian or word processor operator will be able to put your report into a data bank under many headings. People interested in any one of the above subjects will then be able to find and read your report. Without this information retrieval feature, reports or other documents would be seen by only a very narrow circle of readers.

4. Table of contents

The table of contents shows the location of the major headings of the report, so that people can find them. A reader looking for the recommendations should be able to find them listed in the table of contents, together with the page on which they appear. The table will not be necessary for a short report.

Illustrations are usually listed in a separate list, so that a reader can find them more easily.

5. Background (or Introduction)

Some report-writing experts like to call this section the Introduction, but I find this term confusing. When I'm introduced to someone, all that may happen is that names are exchanged, and I learn very little about the person.

The introductory section should provide background to inform any reader who is unfamiliar with the report subject.

47

After reading the background, your reader should know just enough to be able to say:

- I know what the subject is
- I understand why this report was written
- I am interested in reading more.

Again, the secret is to give just the right amount of information to make the reader feel familiar with the subject. This is a difficult thing to do. Most people give too much or too little detail, or drag in facts that should be in other parts of the report. Acknowledgement of help received should be included.

Before you prepare the outline for this section, ask yourself:

(a) Did everything in this section happen before the investigation started?
(b) Are all the verbs in the past tense?
(c) Something started this investigation, but have I said what it was?
(d) Would everyone understand why this report was written, after reading the background?

If any of your answers are no or maybe, think about the outline you have written, remove any items that do not fit, and add what is needed.

6. Investigation

Some people like to call this section the *evidence*, but I think my title is clearer. The investigation is what you do between two milestones:

Milestone 1: You tell yourself or are told to write the report.

Milestone 3: You write the report.

You can probably see that the missing part is:

Milestone 2: You have assembled all the facts, and are ready to work out how they fit together.

In other words, you have *investigated* the problem, but you are not quite ready to reach conclusions. The structure and headings chosen will depend on the subject matter of the report.

The investigation section should tell the reader:

(a) what you were trying to do,
(b) what you actually did,
(c) what you found out.

You should *not* say what conclusions you reached, or what should be done next, as this information belongs in the next section.

7. Conclusions and recommendations
For some reason, in many books on report writing you will see conclusions and recommendations given as two separate headings. The reason usually given is that conclusions don't or shouldn't suggest action, and so a separate section is necessary, after the conclusions.

I don't agree. It can be very difficult to reach a conclusion without a recommendation being buried in it. For example, if you conclude in your report that you have too many people in your company, it seems a little silly to wait for the next section and recommend they be laid off.

In order to write your conclusions and recommendations, look over your investigation section and pick out what you see as major trends in the facts. If you looked at 20 companies, and 10 of them were going bankrupt, it would be reasonable to conclude that something was wrong in this industry. Naturally, after some investigation of the facts, you should know, or be reasonably certain, what was wrong and why. These will be your conclusions. If the recommendations are not obvious, then state what you think should be done. Remember — a report must recommend something to be done, or it is not a report, only a collection of facts. Conclusions and recommendations should have each point numbered if they are extensive.

8. Bibliography
This section is a list of documents you used to prepare the report. An example of how to set out a bibliography follows:

British Standards Institution. *Specification for the Presentation of Research and Development Reports.* (BS:4811. 1972)

Cooper, Bruce. *Writing Technical Reports.* Penguin, 1964.

Davis, Susan, and West, Richard. *Pitman Business English 3: Personal Assistant.* Pitman, 1983.

9. Appendix or appendices (if more than one)
An appendix is a section at the back of a report where you can put supporting information that would be confusing or

overlong if included in the body of the report. The idea is to refer the reader to an appendix for all the information you collected on this topic.

Use appendices as much as possible. Remember that the shorter the main body of the report, the more likely it will be read and acted upon.

All the way through your report, remember who will be reading it. Try to make it interesting for your readers, and anticipate questions that might come up.

Presentation

Because a report is a large document, it has to be packaged in the most interesting way possible, so that it will both be read and be effective. Too often reports are merely filed, and hundreds of hours of the author's time have been wasted. Here are some guidelines.

1. Figures

Use as many tables, charts, diagrams, graphs, schedules, or just plain pictures as you can. Nothing is duller than page after page of text, and your reader will be grateful for any visual relief you can give.

For example, suppose you are suggesting that office space should be reorganised. You could spend many pages describing the moves, or you can say it on one page and refer to an office layout on the opposite page. It is important to have the text and the picture on opposite pages. Nothing annoys a reader more than having to flip backwards or forwards while reading your text.

This type of figure is usually easy and cheap to make. A photocopy of the floor plan with people's names hand-lettered in their locations shouldn't take more than a few minutes of your time. Don't use figures that need professional drawing unless the expense can be justified.

For a more elaborate report, such as one for the shareholders of the company, you may have to use professional artists. In this case, find a book with a figure of the type you want to create and follow its layout. It's a good idea to borrow a good report-writing text and look at its examples.

2. Layout

If your report is going to be acted upon, it is only the first step

Exercise 7.1

Report

Write a report based on the following information:

(a) Your boss (Jones) is on holiday and will be back next week. Jones's boss (Smith) calls you into his office and asks you to prepare some written recommendations for him by next week. He is worried about several things:

1. Your department overspent its budget by 25 per cent last year, and he doesn't want this to happen again.
2. The new budget is now being prepared.
3. No new equipment or people will be allowed for next year, and the money available for your department cannot be more than 110 per cent of last year's figure.

(b) He asks you to think about ways to do the same work in a more efficient way. He wants some ideas on restructuring the department, or better use of the people and equipment, or new techniques which will eliminate time or equipment, or whatever you can dream up. You promise you'll think about it and write down your ideas.

(c) When you get back to your office, you put down these ideas:

1. There are five secretaries in your department, all scattered over the building. If they were grouped together, in a typing pool, one of them might be redundant.
2. Likewise there are four draughtsmen in the same arrangement. How about a draughting pool?
3. The engineering department spends much of its time supervising the production department and solving customer problems with equipment breaking down in the field. Other companies have quality control and repair departments separate from the engineering side. Why not yours?

(d) Looking beyond your own department, you see some cost-saving ideas that might apply throughout the company:

1. There is a large fleet of company cars. Perhaps people could use their own cars and get a mileage allowance while on company business. Insurance might be a problem, however.
2. There is both a large lunchroom and a library, neither of which is much used. How about placing coffee machines in each department, and distributing library material to the interested departments? The space made available could be turned back to the company from which you rent it.

You think that if a large meeting of all department and section heads got together to discuss the overall programme, other cost savings could be realized.

in a long process of discussion and action. Your typewritten pages should have wide left- and right-hand margins and be double spaced, so people can write comments or make changes. Most good reports become discussion papers, and produce results in areas that the author had perhaps not thought of. Your report should be full of good ideas, and your readers may want to apply these ideas to other problems.

3. Follow-up

You should try to make your report a master document, as described in Chapter 8. Who will be the final authority on any decisions you have recommended? How can you make it easy for that person to approve and act on these decisions?

Say that your report recommends a document be sent to someone. Then attach a draft document for approval or signature, just as you did in the memo concerning power supply in Chapter 5. The memo on Mrs Jones is another example. Your memo would eventually reach the departmental head along with your draft letter to Mrs Jones. Try to make your report a complete package in the same way, so that you will not have to prepare any more paperwork.

Suppose you recommend a series of actions in a report, such as a company reorganisation. If you are clever enough to attach a proposed new organisation chart, then all the MD has to do is sign it and the reorganisation is done. If you suggest a series of steps, why not attach a proposed bar-chart schedule? Your MD will most probably be pleased at your ability to think ahead.

Chapter 8
General Tips on Writing Office Documents

This chapter is designed to provide specific writing techniques which can be applied to any document you prepare in the course of your work: memos, letters, or reports.

When you have completed this chapter, you will

- be familiar with the four steps to good writing: outling, sequencing, editing, and paragraphing,
- know the Driver's Seat Test and the Final Sentence Rule,
- understand the importance of tone and effect in your writing,
- eliminate negative, or poison, words or expressions from your writing,
- understand the Master Document Rule.

The four steps to good writing

1. Outlining
How do you outline? Let's take an example. Suppose you are sent by your company to find out about a problem at one of your field offices. You spend a day in the field and come back with several pages of notes. If you hadn't made these notes, you would not be sent on a field trip again, as no one, no matter how clever, can write a satisfactory report from memory.

Your pages of notes are an *outline*, and will probably be a large number of one-line facts or opinions, such as this:

- poor maintenance,
- poor bookkeeping,
- personality clashes between John and George,
- late parts delivery.

The outline you bring back from the trip must now be turned into a report. What is the next step?

2. Sequencing
This is a fancy word for putting everything into some sort of

logical sequence. Perhaps a time sequence is easiest, so use time flow as an organising tool. Remember the time line rule from Chapter 4.

Decide what happened first, next, and last. As you do this, put a number, starting from (1), in front of each fact. This may sound like a trivial thing to do but it is the most important step in writing. If your facts are not organised, very few people will understand your writing. If the facts are in some sort of order, people will understand you, even if your grammar and punctuation are not perfect.

3. Editing

Editing is another word for removing and altering poor material. You might think of a surgeon at work. He or she spends most of the time cutting, and the rest tying things together that were cut in the first place. In between, the surgeon throws out a lot of useless or bad material.

To be a good editor, you need a sharp pencil to cut sentences and paragraphs back to essential ideas, and many of us are too kind to do this. Luckily, most of the time we edit our own material, and we don't have to worry about our own feelings.

Take a paragraph you have written and underline those words that could be used as a heading for the paragraph. These are the *key words* or *phrases*. The idea of editing is to cut back all those words or sentences which do not directly contribute to expressing your essential ideas.

If you are writing about a nuclear explosion in 1945, then in your paragraph the key words are *nuclear explosion* and *1945*. If you find less than one key word per sentence in your paragraph, perhaps you are using too many words for too few ideas. A good rule is:

Find at least one key word per sentence in a paragraph

4. Paragraphing

Once you have identified the key words or phrases they should be organised. The trick is in *how* to organise them.

One good and easy approach is to use time flow. If you have followed the sequencing technique, everything should be arranged in order. All you have to do now is decide where to stop one paragraph and start another.

If you are writing a report, your paragraphing is easy. Put everything that *happened* before you became involved in the project into the first paragraph. Then put everything you

GENERAL TIPS ON WRITING OFFICE DOCUMENTS

found as you looked into the problem into another paragraph. Then, put all *conclusions and recommendations* into a final paragraph.

If your document is long, three paragraphs may not be enough. Then use three major headings, divided into sub-headings or paragraphs.

Every good rule has an exception or two. Sometimes you should put facts down in the order of their importance, rather than the sequence in which they occurred. You will have to think about this when you organise your facts. Generally, time flow is the most natural and effective method, but there are times when other methods are best.

Starting sentences for memos and letters

There is a lot of truth in the saying that first impressions are lasting ones. A good strong start to a piece of correspondence gets your reader on your side. He or she will settle back, convinced that you are going to deal with this subject in an efficient way.

1. The reply

If you are replying to a previous memo or letter, your job is easy. All you have to do is to refer to this previous piece of paper. Here are two examples of good starting sentences of this type:

> *Thank you for your letter of 22 October 198-, asking for information on your insurance policy benefits.*

> *I received your 22 October 198- memo today, and here is the information you wanted on our new computer.*

Notice that this refers to the previous correspondence by date and subject, so that the reader knows exactly what your reply is about. Too often the reader must plough through several paragraphs before it becomes clear why this piece of correspondence was written. If your reader has a bad memory, he or she may never know what you are talking about, and annoyance and frustration will result. Your reader may even have to phone or write you to find out, or worse, will throw the paper away in disgust.

Remember that the single most important thing you can say in the first sentence is *why* you are writing.

2. The Driver's Seat Test

If this memo or letter is the first approach you are making to your reader, the job is slightly more difficult. You will have to catch your reader's interest well enough to keep him or her reading on. How you do this depends on the relationship between you, or what I call the Driver's Seat Test. If you are asking for a favour which can be refused, your reader is in the driver's seat. If you are owed money, and want it, you are driving. Examples of these two situations are:

> *Our department is short of draughtsmen, and our motorway project is falling behind schedule. Could you spare two draughtsmen for two weeks?*
>
> *Your account is £960.37 overdue. Please send us a cheque by 31 October 198-, or we shall have to charge you 2.2 per cent interest per month on the balance.*

Notice who is driving in these examples. The first is *appealing* for co-operation, and the second is *requesting* action. Before you write your first sentence, make sure you know who is driving, and suit the tone and the approach to the situation. For instance, if you need £1,000,000 for a new computer, don't say this in the first sentence of a memo to your boss. Instead, give a short description of the facts or problems that led you to conclude you needed a new computer. This is called *background* information and is vital to make sure your boss will be in the right frame of mind when you finally get around to asking for that million pounds.

On the other hand, if someone owes you money, you don't have to explain quite so much. You should still give some reason for the debt, in case it has been forgotten, and you should be polite, but you can leave out much of the detail.

Final sentences in memos and letters

For some reason, many of us have difficulty in finishing a piece of correspondence. Sometimes a writer will go on and on, like a dinner guest who can't seem to get up the courage to say thanks and leave. Here are some horrible examples at the ends of letters. These are not really sentences, as you will see, but only long-winded ways of saying *sincerely*.

> *Thanking you for your co-operation, I remain,*

First, this is not a sentence. Second, never thank people in advance. They may be annoyed enough to refuse to do what you ask.

Hoping this will receive speedy consideration

Again, this is not a sentence. Worse, it has a begging sound to it, and it uses *speedy*, which is a vague word. If you want a reply by a certain date, say *which* date.

I am, Sir, your most obedient and humble servant, and remain,

I saved this one for the last because I actually had to use it on letters I drafted, to be signed by senior government officials in 1961. No, not 1861, but 1961.

What should the last sentence do?

FINAL SENTENCE RULE
The final sentence in any letter or memo should tell the reader what to do next.

If you want someone to *do* something before 31 October 198-, your final sentence should say

Please send me a cheque for £960.37 by 31 October 1980-.

Any action requested by your memo or letter *must* be stated in your final sentence. If you have asked for help or action in the body of the memo, say it again in the final sentence. Don't worry about repeating yourself. Important messages are worth repeating, as any teacher or person in advertising knows.

Here is a favourite of mine:

If you do not reply before 22 December 198-, I will assume you agree.

This makes the reader of the memo or letter think seriously about what has been read. Silence is the same as agreement, and if your reader doesn't like what you've written, he or she had better speak up. Another less tough approach is:

I hope this will meet your requirements. If not, please reply before 22 December 198-.

Remember, some correspondence is a matter of survival. If you need agreement or action, make sure someone's silence is clearly a vote for your approach. Of course, the person can deny having received your correspondence. As a back-up, phone and make a written record of the conversation. If you send a letter, register it.

Perhaps this is a good time to talk about the *complimentary close*.

These are all acceptable:

> *Yours faithfully,*
>
> *Yours sincerely,*
>
> *Yours truly,*

Remember that your reader will ignore this anyway, and there is no point in wasting much time on it.

Tone and effect

1. Getting the right tone and effect

As you have just seen, the Final Sentence Rule will help you achieve the effect you want from your memo or letter. Other techniques can also help you.

What is meant by the word *tone*? The expression is often used to describe the way someone speaks. We say someone has a certain tone of voice if we want to describe the effect on us. For example, a friendly tone in a conversation encourages us to co-operate with the speaker. An angry tone, however, usually has the opposite result. Tone is the human element in correspondence as well, and if we receive a memo or letter without any tone to it, we suspect the writer is a computer, or a bureaucrat with no heart.

You don't want to sound like this, so how do you put the right amount and kind of tone into your correspondence? Here are some guidelines:

(a) Use only a friendly and helpful tone. Any other could annoy or anger your reader.
(b) Avoid negative-sounding expressions and words. See the next section on poison words.
(c) Think from your reader's point of view. How would he or she like the memo or letter you are sending? Does it answer the question, solve the problem, or help in your reader's work? If it doesn't do any of these, your memo or letter will not have much positive effect.

2. Telegraphing

Once in a while a writer will put down a phrase that makes us wince a little and brace ourselves for something that may annoy us. When a boxer does this, we say he is *telegraphing* his punches. Not many successful boxers can get away with this, and you may want to avoid telegraphing your written punches for the same reason. Some of these warning phrases are useful, but make sure you really want to use them before you write them down.

In the interest of brevity . . .   *In all fairness . . .*

Please rest assured that . . .   *You have every right to . . .*

It is obvious that . . .   *I respect your right to . . .*

. . . is self-explanatory . . .   *I feel it only fair to . . .*

From this, it follows that . . .   *May I take a few minutes of your time to . . .*

With respect, I . . .   *. . . on the assumption that . . .*

Without prejudice . . .   *Contrary to . . .*

You can, I'm sure, add many more to this list, and subtract them from the list of phrases you want to use.

Poison words

We are going to look at a list of words that can sometimes produce a strong emotional response in a reader. There are situations where you can use these words, but you should be careful when you put one in a letter to a client or a customer. These words can be regarded as poison words because, if used in the wrong place or at the wrong time, they can have a poisonous effect.

Many of these words are negative, and might make your reader refuse to do what you want. Telling a customer that he or she *failed* to do something might not encourage that person to do it, for example. Other words can be even more dangerous. If you say

You claim we sent you the wrong valves,

you stand a good chance of making an enemy.

THE BUSINESS WRITING WORKBOOK

Exercise 8.1

Tone and effect

The following paragraphs would probably have a negative effect on a reader. Rewrite them to make them more effective.

1. Please consider me for a job with the Seattle Airplane Company because I really want to be in Seattle. I really haven't any experience in whatever your company is doing, but am so desirous of relocating in Seattle where my family resides, I know I can do very well with your organisation.

2. We very much regret that your application for admission to Sunshine College has been rejected. We have so many good applications from such bright students that we feel we cannot consider yours. If we can be of any further assistance to you, please do not hesitate to let us know.

3. We should like to point out to you that your cheque in the amount of £190.69 is overdue, and that we need your prompt attention to this important matter. We go to a lot of trouble and expense to send out statements and we have creditors of our own. Therefore, you can be of great assistance by putting your overdue cheque in the post.

4. We were most disappointed when your order for convention space did not arrive. May we point out to you that many excellent people signed up for our last convention and reaped many benefits from it. Would you believe over 5000 customers attended this spectacular display of office technology, and over £600,000-worth of orders ensued. For example, a booth 20 foot square costs only £1000.

5. We should like to bring to your attention the fact that we are presently servicing office equipment in your locality. Should you ever feel the necessity for the servicing of such equipment, feel free to contact us and we shall be pleased to hear from you and hopefully we can maintain your equipment on an annual contract basis.

6. Over the past five years we have rewarded our customers who have been doing business with us for more than seven years with a free calculator. As you now qualify, your calculator is on its way, and if you do not receive it, let me know.

7. I was most upset by the comment in your letter that your order was shipped late. This is impossible; we ship the goods the same day. But in your case we are making a special effort to see what happened.

8. Thank you for your recent manuscript submission. Each year our company receives hundreds of manuscripts for evaluation, yet

GENERAL TIPS ON WRITING OFFICE DOCUMENTS

> can publish only a few of them. Regrettably, your material does not fit our present programme, and we cannot consider it for publication. It is returned herewith.
>
> 9. We found it difficult to understand why the modem we sent you last week did not work with your computer. After a little digging we found you ordered the wrong modem. The computer you ordered last year requires a 212 modem but you ordered a 112. If you want the right modem, please let us know.
>
> See examples of more effective paragraphs in the Appendix.

Avoid these poison words and others like them

accident, accidentally   *inadvertent*
argument, argue   *inconvenient*
bad   *ineffective*
believe   *inefficient*
claim (verb)   *late*
complaint, complain   *must*
defect   *overcharged*
delay   *puzzled*
difficulty   *reject*
dissatisfied   *satisfy, satisfied*
enemy   *surprised*
fail   *trust*
faulty, fault   *unaware*
feel   *unfortunately*
hope   *unhappy*
immediately   *wrong*

And any word starting with *un* or *in* or *dis*.

The master document

Many people are in the business of putting information away where others can be sure to find it later. Let's look at what a librarian does as an example. He or she must create a system, so that both of you can find or put away a book in a library. Most libraries use a three-card system, in which each book is referenced on separate author, title, and subject cards.

If you are in a large organisation, you probably do somewhat the same thing. When you write a memo or letter, one copy goes into a subject file, to which you assign a file number.

Another copy goes into a department reading file, usually kept in date sequence. A third copy comes back to you, to be filed in your desk or filing cabinet. This gives you three different ways of finding this piece of paper again.

Look again at the sample memo on power supply (Exercise 5.1 in the Appendix). This memo will end up in three different files, but by tying it to two other documents I have made it even easier to find. The first document is the original note of 1 May 198- which started the investigation. This note is shown as a reference and is summarised in the first sentence of the first paragraph. The second document is the purchase requisition, which is mentioned in the third paragraph and shown as an attachment.

The memo you see has now been linked with the pieces of paper *before* and *after* it. It is easy to find them or recreate them if they are lost. My memo is now the *master document* on this subject, as it organises the paper flow, so that no other piece of paper is as important.

This leads to the *master document rule*. Write your memos and letters as if they were tabled to be the most important part of the paperwork chain. Try to gather in all loose ends, think ahead, and tie your document closely to any paperwork before and after it. In this way, your part of the job will be done well, and your memo, letter, report, or minutes will be the master document.

Many problems which need to be solved suffer from lack of organisation. No one takes charge, and the project drifts on, or dies. If you want a problem solved, or something done, take control when you can, and create a document which will be the master in the chain of paperwork.

Chapter 9
Forms and Manuals

This chapter is designed to give you some useful ideas on how to put together forms and manuals. Some guidelines will be given on form design, and some examples shown. A brief section on manual writing completes the chapter.

When you complete this chapter, you will

- understand the purpose of a useful form and how to design one,
- know the basic techniques of manual writing.

Forms

1. The purpose of forms
Forms are used to handle routine paperwork, or to make sure paperwork is handled in a correct way. If you find yourself writing something out again and again, perhaps you need a form.

Let's look at a very simple example: a routeing slip. Perhaps you already use one, but that doesn't matter. The rules we shall use to invent the routeing slip will apply to other more complicated forms.

Suppose you have to circulate documents regularly to the same people. You may be a supervisor who has to make sure everyone working for you reads new procedures, for example. What are your options?

- (a) You can call everyone into your office and read the procedures aloud. However, some procedures are long or complicated, and need to be studied. Also, what about the people on holiday or off sick?
- (b) You can write across the top of the document *Please circulate* and hope it gets passed to everyone.
- (c) Instead of hoping, you could add everyone's initials to the above. To make sure all have read it, you could add your initials at the bottom, so that the document gets

back to you. Then if someone doesn't follow the new procedure, you can prove that the fault is that person's not yours.

Suppose, however, that your staff members have only crossed out their initials on the document. Could you prove in court that one particular person had read it? Obviously, you need to have each person initial the form. But after writing a dozen or so initials on a number of documents, you might get tired of this routine work, and think of a routeing slip.

2. How to design a form

The routeing slip is one of the most basic forms an office can use. But it reveals some techniques you can learn from the design of even a simple form.

(a) *Design for the person at the bottom*

Any form will probably be filled in by inexperienced or untrained people, so be careful. Don't assume anything. The form should be foolproof.

This, of course, is easy to say, but harder to put into practice. The best approach is to have the most experienced person

---

Exercise 9.1

Routeing slip

Assume that you want a routeing slip for your section of six people. You also want to use the slip to pass documents up the organisation's chain of command. One of your staff may prepare a work order, for example, and give it to the work leader for checking. It then comes to you for your signature, and you pass it to your manager. The manager signs it as approved, and sends it to the financial side of the company, who will check if the money is available to do the work. Perhaps your routeing slip can be attached to work orders and other documents to ensure proper checking and routeing.

Develop such a routeing slip. Make up any names or titles you need, and try to cover as many routine paper transactions as you can think of.

A sample routeing slip is given in the Appendix.

FORMS AND MANUALS

design the form. If you have someone who is an expert in a certain procedure, let him or her produce the form. Also, don't try to produce the final version on your first attempt. Consider the form as a draft for at least six months, and before you have it printed, get the comments of the people who have actually filled it in and processed it.

(b) Think of what can go wrong
One reason for putting a date beside each initial on the routeing slip is that some people delay paperwork. They will be reminded of this by the date, or they can be identified as the bottlenecks, and dealt with.

When the paperwork gets lost, the person finding it needs some way of putting it back into the normal paper flow. If there is a routeing slip, or if the form has good built-in routeing instructions, the form will end up in the right place.

3. The more complicated form

Let's now look at a more complicated form: a purchase requisition. A sample is given on pages 66 and 67.

Following the sample requisition are notes on how to fill in a purchase requisition form. Note the cross-referencing between the text and sample form, by the use of numbers. This can be very effective in documents that require explanation or comment.

The purchase requisition (or PR) is approved by someone with the right financial authority, but who may never have filled in one of the forms, or who may be too busy to check it. It then goes through perhaps dozens of hands until it reaches the buyer in the purchasing department. This person then takes the information off the PR and puts it on another form, called a purchase order.

It is therefore vital that a PR is filled in correctly, and that a set of instructions is attached.

Manuals

You have just seen two examples of form design. The first form needed little or no explanation. The second required a guide, or manual, on how to fill it in. The ideal form requires no guide, but quite often procedures become too complicated to be self-explanatory, and a manual must be written.

THE BUSINESS WRITING WORKBOOK

SAMPLE PURCHASE REQUISITION

Date to be delivered at site[1]	FOB point[2]	Terms[3]		Requisition number[4]		Purchase order number
1 August 198-	Destination			41184		

Vendor's name and address[5]

Division or department[6]

ABC Mfg Ltd
3770 Winston Avenue
Manchester M1 3RB
Attention: F A Lee, Sales Manager

Ship to   Stores[1]
At[7]   120 Pentonville Road, London N1 9JN
Attention   Mr Cliff Ray
Via   Prepaid

Item	Quantity	Unit	Stock no to be quoted	Description of goods or services	Price
1	6	ea		Widgets, in accordance with our Q2-4035 and tenderer's bid 7325, 23 January 198-. or (Lowest bid received) (No substitute, as equipment must be compatible with existing system)	£100.00 ea ESTIP

66

Account distribution			Specific end use of above material is as follows:		
See attached			Generation Control for Mica GS		
Forward copies to I A Stewart	Number 1	Location EG-22	Cost estimate £636	Committed	☐ O/S ☐ BPQ
C Ray	1	Stores 1	PSTIP		Trace date
☐ Copy of PO to Material Standards ☐ Copy of PO to VAT					
☐ Copy of PO to Quality Control and Inspection					

REQUISITIONING DEPARTMENT		MANAGEMENT			PURCHASING DEPARTMENT	
Prepared	Approval to comply with AF-FI	Material Standards	VAT	Traffic	Approvals	Buyer
I A Stewart						
EG-22	Name (print)					
	Signature					
2348	Date February 198-					

PURCHASING DEPARTMENT USE ONLY

Suppliers quoting	Item 1	Item 2	Item 3	Item 4	Item 5	Terms	FOB	Delivery schedule

1. Put realistic delivery date here. If the tender form promises 'six weeks ARO' (after receipt of order) allow three weeks from the time the PR (purchase requisition) leaves your department to issue the purchase order, and then add six weeks to this date. If the tenderer promised 'August 198-', write down this date.
2. If FOB (free on board) point is specified in the tender, leave it blank. If not, better have the purchasing department clear this up before the order is placed. If the tenderer has not yet been selected, put destination. You will be giving a detailed shipping address later.
3. Leave blank.
4. Make sure when you get a copy back for your signature that a requisition number appears here, such as 'No 41184'.
5. Put vendor's full address down, including post code and the name of the sales representative if you have been dealing with one. Put the name after the address like this: 'Attention: Mr E T Jones, Sales Manager'. If you have not yet selected a tenderer, leave vendor off the form.
6. Put your full department name here.
7. Put delivery point in full detail here. In particular, give name to contact.

    The remaining items on the form would be similarly cross-referenced to accompanying notes in the complete guide to the requisition.

In the business and technical worlds, writing a good manual is one of the most difficult jobs. It requires a command of clear and simple English, an expert knowledge of the subject, and an ability to foresee where problems can arise. People with these talents are hard to find, and this is why most manuals are poor.

Let's look at some considerations in writing a manual.

1. Problems in manual writing

Suppose you were asked to write a manual on telephone usage for a remote tribe who spoke and read English, but who had never seen a telephone.

We are all so familiar with telephones that we might think this is a simple exercise. It isn't, of course. I have a 42-page manual written by a student a few years ago which is barely complete.

Many of the problems in writing a telephone manual occur in describing what I call bail-out procedures. These tell you what to do if things go wrong. For instance, three instructions in the manual written by my student are to pick up the phone, put the earpiece to your ear, and listen for the dialling tone. What happens if you don't get a dialling tone? Here are some of the possible problems and corrective actions.

(a) You are listening to the wrong end of the handset. Turn it round.
(b) The phone is disconnected somewhere in the room. Plug it in.
(c) You haven't waited long enough for the dialling tone. Wait at least 20 seconds.
(d) The phone is dead. Find another.
(e) You hear someone talking. Hang up and try again in a few minutes.

These are only a few of the things that can and will go wrong. You will also have to define or describe

(a) dialling tone,
(b) handset,
(c) receiver,
(d) disconnect,
(e) plug,

and so on.

2. Developing an outline

Let's go back to the beginning again. We need a plan or an outline before we start writing things down. Below is a table of contents suggested for our telephone manual.

Section		Title
1.		*General description*
2.		*Specifications*
	2.1	*Mechanical*
	2.2	*Electrical*
3.		*Installation*
	3.1	*Unpacking*
	3.2	*Electrical connections*
4.		*Operating instructions*
	4.1	*Getting a dialling tone*
	4.2	*Dialling a local call*
	4.3	*Dialling a long distance call*
5.		*Theory of operation*
6.		*Adjustments*
7.		*Troubleshooting*
8.		*Schematics, layouts, and parts lists*

Let's look at this section by section.

1. General description

This section tells your reader what the telephone can do. It shows how the instrument fits into society, what it is used for, and why he or she should use it. It explains why this manual exists, and why the reader should read it.

2. Specifications

Though this section is mainly intended for the technical person, it can be useful to the general reader. For example, the mechanical specifications look like this:

> 2.1 *Mechanical specifications*
>   2.1.1   *Weight 1.3 kilograms + 10%*
>   2.1.2   *Impact resistance: 1 metre drop on to concrete*

If you want to despatch a telephone, you would know the approximate weight. If you drop the phone from less than one metre on to concrete, and it breaks, you may be able to claim a replacement.

Specifications also tell your reader how the equipment was supposed to be designed and manufactured. If your unit doesn't meet specifications, something is wrong.

3. Installation

Many equipment problems can be traced to improper installation. Try to think of what can go wrong, and instruct the reader how to install the equipment so that nothing can go wrong.

4. Operating instructions

Remember to include bail-out procedures, such as calling the operator for assistance. Use step-by-step instructions with many pictures.

5. Theory of operation

Like the Specifications section, this is mainly for the technical person, although it can help the general reader understand and eliminate many repair calls.

6. Adjustments

For the normal phone, this section would only describe the

ringer loudness control. For a TV set, of course, this would be the major part of the manual.

7. *Troubleshooting*
This is where a manual can really pay for itself. During the guarantee period, for example, most calls and manufacturer's costs could be eliminated by the equipment user, if he or she can be shown how to locate the problem.

8. *Schematics, layouts, and parts list*
If at all possible, pictures accompanying the written explanations should be right beside the text. Larger and more complicated drawings can be grouped at the back of the manual, mainly to help the person servicing the machine.

Generally, the more pictures, figures, tables, and charts in your manual, the more likely it will be read and followed.

Chapter 10
Meetings

The purpose of this chapter is to teach you techniques you can use to cut down on time spent at meetings, or perhaps avoid them altogether.

Most meetings are a waste of time. They are the curse of the supervisory class. Much of this problem comes from the undisciplined nature of a typical meeting. This chapter will help bring some discipline to your next group exercise in frustration, or meeting.

When you complete this chapter you will

(a) know the Meeting Checklist,
(b) understand agendas,
(c) appreciate the U-Drive Principle,
(d) extend the Master Document idea to minutes of meetings.

The meeting checklist

Over the past 25 years I have gone to more meetings than I can count. I would, however, have no difficulty in adding up on my fingers the number of *useful* meetings I've attended.

After going to four meetings in one day, I became annoyed enough to sit down and analyse why these meetings had gone wrong. These thoughts went into a checklist, and were then used whenever I was forced to run a meeting.

A few years later an article appeared in *Electrical World* magazine that annoyed me almost as much as going to a meeting. I wrote a letter to the editor, and attached the checklist. To my surprise, the letter and checklist were published as an article called 'Cancel That Meeting!' which is reprinted on p.73.

CANCEL THAT MEETING!*

Meetings checklist. Before calling a meeting there are a few axioms you should observe: (1) Avoid all meetings at all costs; (2) Any meeting's potential for disaster is proportional to the number of people present; (3) Hold meetings only when group action is required.

Step 1: Is this meeting necessary? You should ask yourself, can the meeting be eliminated by some combination of personal visits, telephone calls, and paperwork?

Step 2: How to prepare.
- Select attendees carefully. Keep to a minimum — no more than one person from each organisation.
- Ensure that everyone coming can make decisions.
- Telephone everyone and brief them.
- Follow up the phone calls with a written agenda. This written agenda should contain a list of attendees, time, day, date (indicate *Tuesday, 28 Dec*, to be certain) and place of meeting. Remember to spell the names correctly.
- Remember also to brief yourself. Find out all you can about the people at the meeting. After you do this, study each problem to be discussed from their point of view. In addition, collect all previous correspondence, drawings etc, and bring them to the meeting.

Step 3: The meeting. Chair it and write the minutes yourself.
- Have everyone write his or her name and organisation on a piece of paper. Keep the paper.
- Introduce each person, or have them introduce themselves.
- State the purpose of the meeting.
- Ask if anyone has questions at this point.
- Read the minutes of past meetings — if any.
- Keep track of late arrivals — and early departures.
- Take notes of major new information and decisions.
- At the end of the meeting, read the notes out loud, and get agreement.
- Announce the date and agenda of the next meeting (if necessary).

Step 4: Follow-through. Send out summaries of the meeting to the attendees as soon as possible. Remember:
- Keep this communication to one page.
- Make sure that if action is needed, you have said by whom, and by when.
- Avoid emotional language.
- Sign the summary.

Note that minutes should not be a record of everything that went on, but should be merely a summary of important facts, plus decisions reached. If no decisions were reached, you did not have a meeting!

* Reprinted from December 1980 issue *Electrical World* © Copyright 1980, McGraw-Hill, Inc. All rights reserved.

The agenda

They say preparation is the key to success. Meetings may not make you successful, but they can cause you a lot of trouble. You can reduce the chances of a disaster by doing a little work in advance: preparing an agenda. In an earlier exercise on punctuation, we looked at a meeting invitation in the form of a letter. After the corrected punctuation exercise I suggested that the best way of presenting the invitation was by using a special form, and you were given an example. It used headings such as:

> *Place:*
> *Time:*
> *Date:*
> *Subject(s):*   1.
>   2.
>   3.

This is the *only* good way to announce a meeting, and it's called an agenda. Always use headings, as they make it easy for the reader to find the important information, such as the date and subject. If you bury this information in the middle of a memo or letter, don't be surprised if a few people miss the meeting or are unaware of the topic. However, if you make it easy for them to go to your meeting, they'll be there.

If I'm invited to a meeting, I ask for the agenda. If there isn't one, I won't go, unless management insists on it. You too can strike a blow for better and fewer meetings by demanding an agenda. If everyone made this simple and reasonable request, meetings and their costs could be cut by at least half.

The U-Drive Principle

The checklist assumes that you are calling the meeting, and have some choice over who will chair it and take the minutes.

If you want to drive to Birmingham, you could ask someone to take you there. However, that person might not know where you want to go, or how to get there. It is much easier to drive yourself; if you don't get there, you have only yourself to blame. I call this the *U-Drive Principle.*

The same idea applies to taking the minutes, or record, of the meeting. As chairperson of the meeting, you can stop when you want and take notes at your leisure, just like the driver

SAMPLE MINUTES

Subject:
Meeting to Discuss Research & Development Labs Telephone System
Held 25 October 198- at

Present:

H Eddy	R Samuels	TriStar Research
C Kates	A Rabinovitch	& Development
N Barlow	S Owen	
A Matthews		
B Monahan		Titanic Telephone Co
G Carter		
J Brown		Branch office
R Chung		
I Smith		

Background:
Dr Eddy requested the meeting, so that Titanic Telephone and staff could resolve some questions on the future R&D Centre telephone system;

Discussion:

Item	Action By/Date
1. Mr Kates said Titanic Tel has not yet decided what type of equipment it will recommend, until requirements are known. On the other hand, TriStar will not state its requirements until it knows what equipment Titanic has to offer. This is further complicated by Titanic Tel's present investigation of (a) types of electronic PABX to be marketed, (b) costs of same, (c) features to be offered, and (d) sizes of PABXs to meet number of customer stations.	11 Nov
2. Dr Eddy asked I Smith to co-ordinate all R&D telephone requirements by obtaining them directly from the supervisors involved.	I S 1 Nov
3. Ms Chung asked all R&D staff present to complete a questionnaire, which would assist in resolving requirements. After this survey, Titanic Tel would initiate a traffic study.	All staff at meeting 1 Nov
4. Dr Eddy agreed that a common switchboard at Surrey appeared to be a good idea. I Smith and G Carter will still have to discuss this with the department heads now at Surrey	I S & G C 31 Oct
5. As one electronic switchboard located at Surrey Service Centre appeared to be the probable outcome, large conduits in the R&D Centre are not required. System Design has been asked to provide one (1) inch conduits for all telephone facilities within the building. Interbuilding conduit details will be given later.	S O I S 15 Nov

IS/

cc: All present;   L Zimmerman;   B Wing

of a car. As driver, or chairperson, you can hold up discussion until you write down a crucial point. It's your meeting, so run it, and take the notes.

The minutes

A few years ago one of my students told the class that her company never put **CONFIDENTIAL** on any document, as it would be immediately photocopied and dropped on everyone's desk. She insisted, with a straight face, that if the company wanted to keep something quiet, it would be hidden in the minutes of a meeting, as no one ever read the minutes of any company meeting.

How can you make sure your minutes are read, and more important, acted on? The most important thing you can do is think of the minutes as a master document. Quite often, meetings are called to assign responsibilities for a project. In this case, the minutes can be set up to be the master document for the whole project. The trick is to detail each job, assign it to one person, and give a target date for completing it. The minutes now become a working document, which you can use to keep track of the project. The minutes function as the project schedule, without putting the jobs on a bar chart. People hate bar charts, or any other chart. Your best chance of getting them to work to a deadline is to make the minutes of a meeting your working document. (See sample minutes on page 75.)

Chapter 11
The Curriculum Vitae and Letter of Application

The purpose of this last chapter is to give you some helpful ways to improve all the documentation involved in recruiting and being taken on. Some of the most important documents we write are job application letters, cvs and letters of refusal.

When you complete this chapter, you will be able to write better

- cvs,
- covering letters,
- letters of refusal.

The curriculum vitae

The economic recession put many business and technical professionals on the street. Most of them went home, wrote their cvs, and started sending them out to likely companies.

About half of the cvs I see are terrible. They are either poorly typed, ungrammatical, confused and confusing, half-an-inch thick, or look as if they had been done by a professional service, which makes me suspect that the candidate can't write.

How can you prepare a good curriculum vitae?

(a) Don't use a professional service unless you are desperate. There is no substitute for selling yourself. You will have to go into a job interview prepared for questions on your cv, and if you write it yourself, you'll be able to speak with enthusiasm about what is in it.

(b) Don't buy a book on how to write your cv. By the time you finish reading it, several good jobs will have been filled.

(c) If you are working, *now* is the time to write your cv. You have time to think and write, you are not upset or worried, and you probably have access to a good copier. Think ahead and remember Rule 2 from the Introduction to this workbook:

If you are prepared for the worst, it won't happen.

THE BUSINESS WRITING WORKBOOK

The best way to write your cv is to copy the layout of one you like. Below is a typical one which you could use as a model.

SAMPLE CURRICULUM VITAE

Curriculum Vitae[1]

WILLIAMS, James David[2]
125 Bruce Street[3]
Cambridge CB2 5DP

Phone: Home 0223 600 0000
       Office 0223 900 0000

Personal:[4]

Born:	14 November 1945 in Brno, Czechoslovakia
Status:	Single
Height:	5ft 8in
Weight:	11 stone
Citizenship:	British
Languages:	English, Czech, and German

Education:[5]

MSc	Electronics, University of London (Imperial College), 1968
BSc	Electronics, University of London, 1966

Experience:[6]

1970 to present	Senior Design Engineer, Sigma Electronics, Cambridge. Responsible for project group of several engineers and technicians in the area of communication and control system design. Major projects include: design of AC-DC power converters; automated vehicle location systems; automatic radio telephone control head; oil spill detection alarm system; plus a variety of data acquisition systems, including computer interfaces.
1967-69	Project Engineer, high temperature control system for fibreglass curing, Vertex, St Helens, Lancs.

Hobbies:[7]   Computer development, climbing.

THE CURRICULUM VITAE AND LETTER OF APPLICATION

NOTES

1. The document needs a title to show the reader what it is. Most people like to use curriculum vitae, some prefer personal history.
2. Put your last name first, in capitals, followed by a comma and your forenames as shown. Underline the name you are known by.

    All this is very important if your last name looks like a forename or if it's foreign. A mix-up at this stage could be disastrous, as your cv could be filed by the personnel department under the wrong name.
3. Put your full address and both home and office telephone numbers here. Don't forget the area code, as looking this up might annoy someone trying to reach you. Make it easy for that person.
4. I like a personal section because it builds up a picture of the applicant in my mind. Some people argue that this information is none of anyone's business, but it will probably come out sooner or later. If, however, you are five feet tall and weight 20 stone, don't put this down. A cv should only emphasise your good points. Leave out anything negative. It's up to the interviewer to find out about your weak spots. A cv is your advertisement, and your goal is to obtain an interview. You should also omit your age if you are under 25 or over 45.

    Put down your citizenship only if you are naturalised. This shows you are committed to your new country.

    Any second or third languages could be very useful to an employer. Leave out this part if you are unilingual.
5. Put your most recent education first. Your most recent education or training is freshest in your mind, and is more important than a 20-year-old diploma. Don't go back to A levels or CSEs unless this is as far as you went. Put down continuing education courses, as they show initiative.
6. Again, list your most recent experience first, as it should be the most important. Put down . . . *to present* to save you changing the cv each year. This will also be useful if you become unemployed.

    The experience section is the most carefully read. Be sure to put down:
    (a) your title, if you had one,
    (b) number of people you supervised, if any,
    (c) major projects. Did you do something worthwhile while you were there? Describe it.
7. Be careful about hobbies. Those that are work-related are fine, but the person who lists more than three makes me wonder how serious he is about work.

General

Like any other document, you should try to keep it to one page. This is hard to do after 30 years in the business, but resist the temptation to tell people in detail what you did 30, 20, or even 15 years ago. They probably will not be interested.

Minor gaps can be concealed by using the years without naming the months. If you took a year off and hitch-hiked through North

> Africa, this looks bad to some people. I can't recommend that you lie about it, but if you worked as a cook or dishwasher during this period, why not stretch things a little? Your job is to sell yourself, while the personnel department is trying to weed you out of a field of applicants. Why give them an unimportant fact that allows them to reject you? Say, for example:
>
>   1970   Dishwasher, Hotel Abuweyel, Algiers, Algeria

The covering letter

Before writing a covering letter, check to make sure your cv covers the job on offer. Are there any qualifications which you have not emphasised, but which appear to be key requirements? Then play these up in your covering letter. The letter should amplify or add to your cv, where necessary. If the cv fits the job perfectly, of course, all the letter has to say is that you are applying for the job, and your cv is attached.

Have a look at the sample covering letters which follow. These will help you to write your own covering letters.

SAMPLE COVERING LETTER (1)

> 6055 Montague Avenue
> Evergreen
> Warwickshire CV23
> Date

First-Rate Management
1 Winner's Circle
Milton Keynes MK9 2HL

Dear Sir or Madam

I am attaching my cv in response to your weekend *Investor* advertisement. As you can see, I might fit into several of the senior management areas you mentioned, particularly in the aerospace electronics field.

   Though I am heavily involved in several major Titanic Telephone projects, involving replacement of much of our 2000-mile-long microwave system and purchase of our countrywide telephone system, I can see no further major projects on the horizon.

   I could be available for interview at any time.

Yours faithfully

Robert A Capulet

SAMPLE COVERING LETTER (2)

18 Upward Avenue
Manchester M16 5RB

Tel: Office 061-687 0000
     Home 061-876 0000

Date

Personnel Officer
In-Depth Research Ltd
Stockport SK6 8DX

Dear Sir or Madam

I am applying for the position of Technology Adviser, as advertised in Saturday's *Researcher*. My cv is attached.

In addition to the information in the cv, I have for some years acted as an unofficial adviser for several companies. In fact, I have written many grant applications for these companies, including:

1984	—	Proposals for High-Tech Electronics' vehicle location, power conversion and mobile radio projects.
1983	—	Proposal for Sea Systems, for a grant to develop a high-powered SSB low-frequency communication system for undersea use.
	—	A proposal grant for Dynamic plc's microprocessor-based low-voltage high-power supply.
1980	—	A proposal for a micro-based theatre lighting and dimmer system for Luxor Lighting.
1979	—	A proposal for a modular concrete building system for Modern Building Ltd.
1978	—	A micro-based proposal for Sharp-Shock Electronics for a grant.
	—	A proposal to develop printed circuit-type jackfields incorporating alarm and indication, for Wizard Electronics Ltd.

Most of these proposals were funded by the Department of Trade and Industry and many resulted in successful products.

I would be more than pleased to furnish further information or to meet for an interview.

Sincerely,

Rodney Longscope

THE BUSINESS WRITING WORKBOOK

Exercise 11.1

Curriculum vitae and covering letter

(a) Write your cv, using the sample as a basis.
(b) Then write a covering letter to an organisation that might be looking for someone like you. Find an ad in the paper or make up a typical job opportunity.

Make your letter interesting and informative, and it will help you get selected by the personnel department for an interview.

Turning down a job offer

Often we have to admit we've made a mistake or take back what we said. This is bad enough, but it becomes really painful when we have to write it down. Because we all have a large amount of pride, some of us become emotional and have great difficulty in choosing the right way to say 'I was wrong' or 'I can't do as I promised'.

Exercise 11.2

Letter of refusal

Let's say you applied for a job at the ABC Corporation. You were interviewed, wined, dined, and offered the job. You accepted.

Then the XYZ Company offers you a better job, with more money and responsibility. You accept that offer, but now you have to write to ABC and explain what happened.

Write a polite letter, making up any details you need to make the letter sound true to life.

See the Appendix for a sample letter of refusal.

Appendix

Exercise Answers

Exercise 2.1

Vocabulary reduction

1. free, natural easy
2. erase, remove
3. regular, orderly
4. cool, calm, mild
5. wary, cautious, alert
6. repay, compensate
7. inexcusable, unforgivable
8. soft, flabby
9. free, immune
10. implied, understood
11. clear, plain, spelled out
12. obvious, clear, plain
13. root out, destroy, remove
14. false, wrong, mistaken
15. route, trip, journey
16. vague, doubtful, uncertain
17. right, reward, tip
18. supreme, chief
19. finicky, fastidious, hard to please
20. error, deception

Note
The answers are only suggestions. The right equivalent depends on how the word is used in a sentence. If your answers are different, you might check them in a thesaurus or dictionary.

THE BUSINESS WRITING WORKBOOK

Exercise 2.2

Shortening sentences (1)

1. ~~If you want~~ For more modern equipment, ~~you will have to~~ go to a larger manufacturer~~, that is larger in size~~.
2. Without these important qualities, you will ~~be nothing but a~~ failure as ~~far as being~~ a manager~~. goes~~.
3. The ~~nature of the~~ calculations ~~needed to arrive at~~ for a good office design ~~is outlined~~ are on page 60.
4. The two lists came to ~~a total sum of~~ £479.
5. Please ~~bring~~ hasten this file~~, to a hasty conclusion~~.
6. The car's engine was running ~~at a high rate of speed~~ fast.
7. On ~~the date of~~ 4 June ~~we shall begin plant operations~~ the plant starts up.
8. ~~This~~ I prefer this recommendation~~, is found to be preferable by myself~~.
9. The ~~excavation~~ hole ~~depth~~ was ~~great~~ 1 metre deep.
10. We saw ~~a large number of people working at their desks~~ many office workers.
11. ~~The majority of~~ Most serious accidents ~~have~~ occurred during peak ~~times when~~ traffic ~~activity was at a peak~~.
12. Any ~~of the building~~ plot will ~~be dimensionally capable of accommodating~~ take house design number 31.
13. Acorn Industries has ~~made many~~ reorganised ~~organizational changes needed to be made in order for it~~ to become a better company.
14. ~~In accordance with your request~~ As requested, attached ~~please find~~ is our financial statement ~~giving sales volume prior to the date~~ of 12 February 1985.

Exercise 2.3

Shortening sentences (2)

1. All these events should be listed in ~~the consecutive~~ order~~, in which they occurred~~.
2. Switzerland ~~is another~~ 's winter sports ~~country that~~ attracts visitors.
3. All the tins were ~~closed, so that the~~ air tight ~~could not touch the contents~~.
4. Cornflour ~~is a food that~~ can be easily dissolved ~~in liquid~~.

APPENDIX

5. This insect is ~~so small that it is seen only by looking through a~~ microscop~~e~~ic.
6. The road sign was ~~located~~ at the ~~place where the two roads~~ intersect~~ed~~ion.
7. We should ~~thoroughly~~ discuss ~~the question as to~~ whether we should leave today.
8. Dogs ~~are animals that can~~ eat every type of food.
9. Petrol ~~is a liquid that~~ can ~~or will~~ be easily ignited.
10. ~~The fact that we have received~~ Our diplomas indicate/s progress.
11. My Italian next-door neighbours, ~~who came from Italy,~~ are applying for their naturalisation papers tomorrow.
12. The ~~place for which the~~ boat's destination ~~was headed~~ was kept secret from us.
13. ~~Now~~ There ~~there~~ is a meeting ~~going on~~ in Suite 200.
14. Instead of stopping, the taxi driver ~~made the cab go~~ went faster.
15. The ~~story told by the~~ lawyer's story was ~~impossible to believe~~ unbelievable.
16. She was ~~possessed by a desire to achieve a high station in life.~~ Many ambitions.
17. ~~The~~ Many floors were too cold ~~for comfort in many cases~~.
18. ~~Using a~~ Use computer keyboard, ~~you should exercise~~ a light touch on the keys of a computer.
19. The computer, ~~which was unheard of as late as the 1940s,~~ has changed ~~the face of~~ business ~~activities~~.
20. ~~It is extremely rare that a~~ A mistake is rarely made in counting the church collection.

Notes to Exercise 2.3

Many new versions of the sentences in this exercise are shorter and better than the originals. There is no one correct answer.
    Let's look at some of the trickier ones.

Sentence 1.
It can be argued that the events can be listed in several ways, for example alphabetically, or in order of importance. But the most natural sequence is that of time, and 99 people out of 100 would pick this meaning above all others.

Sentence 3.
Is a sealed tin air-tight? Some people think so, but others may disagree. You could say: *The tins were vacuum sealed.*

Sentence 7.
Here you might say: *We should discuss our departure tomorrow.* However, this leaves out the information that there is some doubt as to whether they will leave or not.

Sentence 8.
Another possibility is: *Dogs are omnivorous.* However, very few people would know this word.

Sentence 15.
Unbelievable has five syllables and is hard to spell, but it's a very good word. *Incredible* would also be a good choice.

Sentence 17.
Some floors were too cold is wrong. *Some* is less than half, while *many* is more than half.

Sentence 19.
The phrase that has been cut has almost no meaning. If you insist, you could say: *The invention of the computer...*

Exercise 2.4

Reducing standard phrases

1. In the normal course of our procedures
   Omit

2. We have discontinued the policy of
   We don't, have stopped, no longer

3. Therefore we ask that you remit
   Please send, remit, pay, return

4. Will you please arrange to send
   Please send

5. We are of the opinion that
   We or I think

6. In view of the fact that
   Omit

APPENDIX

7. Will you be good enough to
   Could you please
8. At all times
   Omit
9. In regard to
   Omit
10. In the near future
    Omit
11. In view of the above
    Omit
12. In the amount of £100.49
    £100.49
13. Under date of 6 June
    On 6 June
14. The facts of the matter are
    Omit
15. In the event that
    Should, if, in case
16. At the present time
    Now, currently
17. In advance of
    Before, prior to, ahead of
18. Come to a decision
    Decide, determine
19. Grant approval
    Approve, let
20. Come to an end
    End, finish, stop, cease
21. Owing to the fact that
    Because, since, as
22. Make a revision
    Revise, correct, change
23. I was unaware of the fact that
    I didn't know

24. In spite of the fact that
Although, in spite of, though

25. He is a man who
He

26. As soon as possible
Omit

Notes to Exercise 2.4

Of all the weeds in our language, the phrases in Exercise 2.4 are the worst. You have probably seen them so many times that you don't notice them any more. If you put them in your own letters, you do so automatically.

What they say is either so obvious or trivial that they should be left out.

Phrase 1.
If you do something in a normal way, you wouldn't expect someone to comment on it. If a bank, for example, writes to you and says, *In the normal course of our procedures*, they are saying that they found something while they were working in a normal way. As we all expect banks will behave in a normal way, we are not made happy by being told the obvious. If it is obvious, why say it?

The same principle applies to Phrases 6, 8, 9, 10, 11, 14 and 26.

Phrase 5.
We are of the opinion that . . . Often the writer who says this is hiding behind the word *we*. Actually this is the writer's opinion, but the writer is hoping you won't challenge his or her claim to speak for the organisation in question. This phrase should be: *I think* . . .

However, the *we* is acceptable if you really do speak for your company.

Phrases 10 and 26.
As these phrases do not specify *how much* time, they contain no information and should be omitted.

APPENDIX

Exercise 3.1

Dangling phrases

1. My bank balance improved after I talked to my accountant.
2. While Julia was on her lunch hour, her child fell out of the tree and was rushed to the hospital by the school nurse. The child may have a fractured arm.
3. As I walk down Hastings Street, the new hotel towers above the other buildings.
4. The police officer arrested the reckless driver.
5. I prepared the specimen for the lab after soaking it in alcohol for one day.
6. These forms will be useful to you as an employee in our company.
7. Egypt's six-year-old administration, headed by Mubarak, has done much to advance the cause of peace in the Arab world.
8. After the game, Wayne Gretsky received another award for scoring.

Exercise 3.2

Punctuation

8 April 1985
Mr John W Smith
General Manager
Intercontinental Services Ltd
2055 Main Road
Westview, Wiltshire

Dear Mr Smith

Thank you for your letter of 6 March which we have just received. It must have been delayed by the mail strike.

The conference has been rescheduled for the weekend of May 23/24 inclusive. It will be held at the Landmark Hotel, 25 Robert Street. Our guest of honour, Ms Shirley Jones will deliver a major speech at 8 pm on Friday the 22nd. Her topic will be Women in Advertising. The delegates will also hear panels on the following topics: Current Problems in Advertising; The Challenge of

Consumerism; and New Marketing Trends. It promises to be a lively and interesting meeting. If you still wish to attend, please send your cheque for £25 to cover registration fees and add £10 if you wish to attend the banquet Saturday night, gratuity included. We look forward to seeing you. Please accept my apologies for the delay in answering your letter.

Yours sincerely
Thomas A Weston
Information Director
Advertising Council

Notes to Exercise 3.2

This exercise is intended to show you how difficult it is to punctuate and how many different ways are acceptable. This should make you want to *avoid* punctuation whenever you can.

This letter would be far better as a form announcement, like this:

Conference announcement

Date:	22-24 May 1987
Time:	8 pm
Speaker:	Ms Shirley Jones
Topic:	Women in Advertising
Cost:	£25 per person plus £10 if you wish to attend the banquet

Please send cheque in advance to:

See how easy it is to find the important facts in this piece of paper. Also, the form can be used for the next conference. Many letters can be avoided by using forms.

Exercise 4.1

Eliminating the passive coice

1. None of the above was understood by anyone.
   No one understood the above.

APPENDIX

2. The undersigned was not contacted by your office.
   Your office did not contact me.

3. It has frequently been suggested by our company that your expenses are tax deductible.
   Our company has often suggested that your expenses are tax deductible.

4. This programme has been neglected by many of our viewers, who have been annoyed by its contents.
   Many of our viewers have neglected this programme because they have been annoyed by its content.

5. In certain circumstances, we have been asked by our customers to give discounts.
   Our customers have asked us to give discounts in certain circumstances.

6. May we suggest that we not be asked to consider these alternatives at this time.
   We do not wish to consider these alterations at this time.

7. This government has been asked by its many critics to cancel its aid to this nation.
   Many critics have asked this government to cancel aid to this nation.

8. I have been approached by many of our creditors to relax our penalty charges.
   Many of our creditors have asked me to relax our penalty charges.

9. When two interest payments have been applied and not met, often the payment schedule has been abandoned.
   The payment schedule has often been abandoned when two interest payments have been applied and not met.

10. The computer has not been received with much favour in some industries.
    In some industries the computer has not met with much favour.

Exercise 4.2

Parallel structure

1. Mr Johns is a man of integrity and achievement.
2. I told Steve to spend more time working and less time visiting.
3. The manual is out of stock and out of print.
4. He said he would return soon and we should work hard while he was away.
5. In the civil engineering course, every student learns how to use a theodolite and survey a property.
6. Jack's job is promoting computers and selling the company image.
7. The salesman's talk was long, boring, and inaudible.
8. I like watching football and soap operas on TV.
9. Our library is an excellent place for research or casual reading.
10. Jack asked me to stop at the supermarket and pet shop on my way home.

Exercise 4.3

Subject and verb agreement

1. We have lost five pounds.
or A five-pound note is missing.
2. No committee member has wanted to charge for personal expenses.
3. It seems that one of us has to do all the work.
4. Both candidates lack promise.
or Neither candidate is promising.
5. Each jury member has selected his or her hotel room.
or The rooms have been selected by each jury member.
6. At the head table we see a couple called Peters.
or The Peters are at the head table.
7. We have spent £200 of our fees.
8. We are going with one of the twins.
or One twin is going with us.

9. The hard part is pulling and pushing.
10. We see a man and a woman standing on the field.

Exercise 4.4
The time line (1)

Leave the first two paragraphs as they are.

    Zurfluh's vehicle was seen weaving down the motorway by Pc Bill Robinson. Zurfluh ran from his vehicle, was collared, and put into a patrol car.

    The 18-year-old from Stettler ripped the crotch out of his undershorts as he sat in the car, stuffed the fabric in his mouth, and then spat it out. Later, a breath analysis showed his blood alcohol level was exactly at the legal limit of .08 milligrams per 100 millilitres. He was acquitted on a charge of impaired driving by Judge David MacNaughton.

    Students from a local high school, in court to view the workings of the law, had difficulty maintaining their composure when the testimony grew lively, and were removed by their teacher.

    'People were leaving the courtroom with tears in their eyes', said Constable Peter McFarlane.

Exercise 4.5
The time line (2)

Our new word processor installation should go smoothly if we follow this sequence of events. First, the board of directors should be asked to approve the £20,000 purchase. As the machine is available in eight weeks, training of two secretaries at XYZ Business College should start immediately after approval. Also, our accounts department should be given the new system manuals so that our procedures will be compatible with the new filing system. After the system is installed, our sales brochures should be rewritten by our sales department to let our customers know we have this new service to offer.

Exercise 5.1

Short memo

Memorandum

Memo: Mr P E Jones[1] Date: 8 May 198-[2]
From: A R Williams File: 2-08-12[3]
Subject: 1 BX2 Power Supply Problems[4]
Reference: Your note of 1 May 198-[5]

In your note, you described a problem we were having with the 1 BX2 power supply. Several times a day, and immediately after the load was connected, the supply output fuses were blown.[6]

The load is too large for the supply. When the load is connected, it draws 10 amperes, and the five-ampere supply fuse blows.[7]

I recommend buying a 20-ampere supply. A purchase requisition for a Tambda XC-20 is attached for your signature.[8]

Enclosure: PR 12369[10]   A R Williams[9]

Notes to exercise 5.1

1. It is optional whether you put Mr, Mrs, or Ms before your reader's name; use all initials. You could use a title or a location if he or she is in another department or area.
2. This is a clear and short way of writing the date.
3. A file number allows this memo to be correctly filed. This is a memo for the record, so you must file it where anyone can find it.
4. The subject should be a short summary of the memo.
5. Many people are surprised and worried by a memo. If you can show them they asked you to send it, they will be happier about reading it.
6. This paragraph is the background statement. It tells the reader what happened before you looked into the problem. Notice the past tense.
7. This is the investigation section. You did some measurements, so include the data. Notice the present tense.

APPENDIX

8. This is your recommendation. It asks your superior for *action*. In this case, all he has to do is sign the attached purchase requisition, which then automatically goes to the purchasing department.
9. Sign your name here. A signed memo shows you read it and certified it was correct.
10. Put 'Enclosure' and the serial number if you are attaching a document.

Note that I have left out any mention of the damage I caused by putting in larger fuses. This foolish action can be compared to putting pennies behind the fuses in your house electrical panel. If you can avoid it, don't confess in writing to stupidity.

Exercise 5.2

Memo report

Here are a few examples of good and bad ways to write this memo.

(a) During my investigation, I reviewed:
   1. The company rules and regulations on dismissal.
   2. The company rules on medical insurance.
   3. The employment record of Mr P J Jones — File 16825.

It's obvious that someone investigating the problem would do all this. Omit.

(b) 1. Company regulations follow employment law.
   2. Company rule 567 states: The widow of a pensioned employee shall be entitled to a pension and medical insurance in accordance with the contract of employment at the time of retirement.

Excellent. If you can, quote a rule or regulation that says what to do. Quote it in full or in part, or attach it as an appendix.

(c) As requested verbally by you on 20 December, I investigated Mrs P J Jones's complaint that her husband's medical insurance did not appear to cover her imminent operation. The letter is attached. The question of correct entitlement arises from Mr Jones's early retirement enforced by his misconduct, when the company did not

97

> exercise its usual prerogative of granting medical
> insurance to his dependants after his death; his pension
> was paid in full, however, which the company had no
> obligation to do, but it was not index-linked. He died in
> a car accident in April 1985.

The last three sentences are part of the investigation, while the first part is background.

> (d) *Recommendation*
> Mrs Jones should be advised that the situation as stated by the medical insurance company is correct and that no change will be made. Attached is a draft letter for your comments or action.

Excellent.

> (e) Our medical insurance company have quoted for Mrs Jones to rejoin the scheme as a private individual. The quote is attached.

I think this information should be part of the memo report, even though it is not the company's responsibility.

> (f) Mrs P. Jones, the widow, has heard that her late husband's medical insurance does not cover her operation. She infered that an error had been made.

The major error here is the lack of specific reference to Mrs Jones's letter. We don't know whether she phoned, visited, or wrote. If she wrote, you *must* give the date of the letter, as you could have received many letters from her.

Note the word *inferred* has been spelled wrongly and is the wrong word to use. Rare words are hard to spell and understand. *Suggested* is the right word.

> (g) Two alternative courses of action can be considered:
> 1. Mrs Jones can be informed that no error was made and that the change in her husband's circumstances was the result of his misconduct.
> 2. The company could agree to cover the costs of Mrs Jones's operation.
>
> Any changes to the insurance could imply that an error was made by the department. Since Mrs Jones is receiving a pension, she could attempt to take legal action to claim the accompanying 'free' medical insurance.

APPENDIX

Fine, but a concluding statement such as *I therefore recommend Option (1)* is needed.

> (h) *I recommend that we tell Mrs Jones the circumstances under which her husband was pensioned off.*
>
> (i) *It seems unlikely that Mrs Jones did not know of the circumstances since they were living together at the time and her husband must have been showing signs of strain.*

Good.

> (j) *I recommend that nothing be done since the company is in the right.*
>
> *However, Mrs Jones may elect to join the medical insurance scheme at her own expense. Since she needs an operation, the contribution is likely to be very high.*

Exercise 6.1

Letter

Date: 10 April 198-
File: 856-786

Dear Mrs Jones

Thank you for your letter of 10 March 198-.

You asked me why your husband's medical insurance does not extend to you in your widowhood. The attached extracts from his personal file will, I hope, show you that the company was not obliged to continue his medical insurance after he left, in view of the circumstances of his retirement.

Yours sincerely

Personnel Manager

Enclosure

Exercise 6.2

Rejection letter

Dear Ms Shannon

Marketing Manager position

Thank you for your prompt reply to our advertisement.

Yours was but one of the over 100 interesting cvs we received. Because of this excellent response we were able to select candidates with exactly the right qualifications and experience.

Although we won't be considering your application for this position we will certainly keep your cv on file for three months in case a more suitable position opens up.

We appreciate your interest in ABC Insurance and wish you well in your future career.

Yours sincerely,

John S Duncan
Personnel Officer

Exercise 8.1

Tone and effect

1. Would your Seattle office be looking for a young woman, who has little experience in the aeroplane business but is not afraid of hard work? I would like a junior position in your engineering environment in the United States, where I can learn to apply what I have been taught at Cranfield.

2. I am sorry, but all our classes in Business Administration are filled.
   Perhaps you could apply to us next year, or better still, you might contact the colleges on the attached list. As recently as last week, two or three of them still had openings.

3. Please send your cheque for £190.69 before 30 September 1987. After September, an interest charge of 2 per cent per month will be added to your bill.

APPENDIX

4. We have a bargain for you on the rental of a booth at this year's Office Automation Convention. For example, a 20 by 20 foot booth costs only £1000 for four days of display time.
    Last year 5000 people attended and placed over £600,000-worth of orders. This year we expect over 10,000 customers and more displays. Please reserve your space before 7 October 1987, as we are almost fully booked.

5. May we introduce ourselves? Alpha Equipment is now servicing typewriters, word processors, and electronic copiers in Manchester, as well as in Liverpool, Leeds and Bradford. We should be delighted to quote on your servicing needs, either on a single repair, or on an annual contract.

6. As you have been such a good customer for the past five years, I am sending you a calculator to show my appreciation. If you have not received the calculator by 30 May, please let me know.

7. I am sorry our order was late. I have asked the shipping company, Moonlite Express, to give us a report on why this happened.
    Note. This letter should be attached to a copy of the despatch note, bill of lading, or packing slip.

8. Thank you for sending us your business writing manuscript.
    We enjoyed reading it, but as we do not usually publish this type of material, we sent the manuscript to our associates at Diligent Press. You should soon be hearing from them.

9. Thank you for your letter of 10 May describing your problem with our 112 modem. We checked the computer you bought from us last year, and it requires a 212 modem. A 212 has been shipped to you today. When you receive it, please return the 112 and we will invoice you for the difference.

Exercise 9.1
Routeing slip

ROUTEING SLIP[1]			
Initial, record date, and forward			
	Initial	*Date*	*Routeing*
G Bell			
D Knight			
S Sainsbury			
D Greenwood			
W Heinz			
A McArthy			
I A Stewart			
─────── [2]			
Department Manager			
Controller			
Secretary			
File[3]			

Notes to Exercise 9.1

1. You need a title on the form so that people will know what it is. The instructions on how to use it are the headings at the top of each column. If you wanted all people in the section to see the document and return it to you, you would simply write in the routeing column the numbers 1 to 7, starting at the top. If you are S Sainsbury and you have just prepared a work order, you would put your initials and the number *1* on the slip, and give it to your work leader, G Bell, who completes the routeing and initials the slip, showing that your work was checked. The document and slip then go to the supervisor, department manager, and controller in turn.

2. Leave some blank spaces for other people's names. If some

of your people leave, you can still use the form, if you leave room for their replacements.

3. You may not want to see the material again, but would like it filed by the secretary.

Exercise 11.2

Letter of refusal

You have to be honest with the ABC Corporation. The person who selected you will be disappointed and upset that you have changed your mind. He or she deserves a full explanation.

I recommend giving ABC details of the better job with XYZ, including the amount of money and responsibilities. Some people object to this, saying that it sounds as though you are trying for more money. The point is that there *is* a job market, and if you are worth £5,000 more than ABC offers you, ABC will be most interested to know this. It will help them in placing their next ad for this position, for example. And if they phone you and offer £10,000 more, what harm is there in that? You are selling yourself, and they are buying.

Here is an example.

Dear Bob

I very much enjoyed the dinner last week with you and your charming wife Julia. Your job offer was most interesting, and I was looking forward to joining the ABC Corporation.

Unfortunately, yesterday I received and accepted another offer from the XYZ Company. As their position offers more responsibility and a 20 per cent higher salary, I could not turn it down. I hope you will understand and pass on my regrets to all those in your company who interviewed me.

Please accept my apologies for all the trouble you have taken on my behalf. Our meeting was so pleasant that I hope our paths will cross in the future.

Yours truly

Samantha Jones

Samantha Jones

Further Reading from Kogan Page

The Business Guide to Effective Speaking, Jacqueline Dunckel and Elizabeth Parnham, 1985

The Business Guide to Effective Writing, John Fletcher and David Gowing, 1987

Readymade Business Letters, Jim Dening, 1986

The Secretary's Survival Manual, Sandra Tomkins, 1986

The Word Processing Handbook, John Derrick and Phillip Oppenheim, 1984

Wordpower, Neil Wenborn, 1981

Writing for a Living, Ian Linton, 1985